This book is dedicated to all of those who helped it grow to be what it is or ever will be. Particularly I'd like to thank Ellen of the well for the crazy idea in the first place. Also Debra, who can spell; Francine, my favorite musical idiot; Marcus, who built and later resurrected my guitar; Jay, the supreme perfectionist; Cousin Dave, who can also spell; the special folks at Woodvale—Linda, April, Bob and Ron, who put up with me and my typewriter; Mom who gave me life (a favor I still appreciate); Charles, local magician with pen; and my editor, Paul Abrams, who isn't so bad with a pen himself.

But more than anyone, this book is for Lisa Cron who converted it from an interesting idea into thousands of copies of what you now are reading. Without her determination to show folks this isn't just another guitar book nobody would have read the manuscript. Profound thanks.

the GuitarOwners Manual

BUYING, REPAIRING & MAINTAINING AN ACOUSTIC GUITAR

by Will Martin

John Muir Publications   *Santa Fe, New Mexico*

Published by: John Muir Publications
              P.O. Box 613
              Santa Fe, New Mexico 87501

Illustrated by Charles Peale

Library of Congress Cataloging in Publications Data:

Martin, Will, 1954-
    The guitar owner's manual.

    1. Guitar.   2. Guitar—Repairing.   I. Title.
ML1015.G9M37 1983   787.6'12   83-8208
ISBN 0-912528-30-3

CONTENTS

The
Guitar Owner's
Manual

Preface

I've spent lots of time with guitars. I've owned many, worked closely with some very fine instrument builders and repair-people, and I've taught thousands of people more than they probably ever wanted to know at the Musical Instrument Maker's Shop in Colonial Williamsburg, Virginia.

My experience with guitars ranges from the ecstacy of composing music on a wonderful guitar that felt just right, to the agony of realizing I had just backed the car over my guitar case. I've fine-tuned the playing action of exquisite handmade guitars, and I've torn the necks off cheap guitars to fix them and make them play again.

When John Muir Publications publishes one of its famous automobile books, it finds (or is found by) an expert who has worked on a specific car for years and knows it inside and out. The writer then converts those years of experience into a book that's packed with information, encouragement and friendly guidance. Finally, all the procedures are tested by non-experts (fondly referred to as "idiots") to be sure it is all do-able. My book about guitars is intended to carry on in that spirit.

In this book, I will give you shortcuts toward understanding what it took me ten years to accumulate. You will learn how to evaluate any guitar you meet, in terms of how well it suits the music you want to play, and what care, adjustments, or repairs it needs to stay in tip-top shape. For those who want to do their own repairs and adjustments, I tell you how. Seeking a good, experienced luthier is the safest method of all. Sometimes it's absolutely essential, but, even when you take your guitar to a pro, the more you understand it the better you will be able to discuss the adjustments or repairs you need done.

So, let's begin this greater understanding of a great musical instrument...

Will Martin

CHAPTER 1

What is a Guitar?

It sounds like a stupid question, but recognizing a guitar when you see one is not the same thing as knowing what a guitar is. To complicate matters, people keep coming along with new designs that stretch the definition of guitarness. For the sake of brevity and my lack of expertise, this book will not discuss in detail those electronic wonders which produce nary a sound without being plugged in. Perhaps in the future my education will enable me to write *The Electric Guitar—An Owner's Manual*, but for now, I know a flanger from a humbucker, and perhaps a little more, but not enough for the definitive work.

I was once taught that we can perceive things only by discontinuities. That means that if you walked into a room where this book was on a coffee table, it would be easy to find because the book would look very different from any part of the table. If you entered my room and this book was on my desk, you might never notice it, because my desk is *covered* with things that look a lot like this book. The book would blend right into what you would perceive as a pile.

That's what it's like when looking at a guitar for the first time. The different parts of the guitar may go totally unnoticed because you don't see a nut, saddle, bridge, bouts, heel, etc. You see a guitar, and that's all you see.

If you don't own a guitar yet, try to borrow one before reading the next section so you can explore the instrument, learning what the different parts look, feel and smell like. If your guitar differs drastically from the illustrations here, skip to those of Jazz guitars, Dobros and the like on pages 28-29.

A Tour of the Guitar

As you read this, refer to the illustrations to help find the different parts of the guitar you've got at hand. Learning the terminology now will help you greatly through the rest of the book.

People tend to personify things they love, so many parts of the guitar are named after human parts. The **body** is the big part with all the curves. The **head** (also called the **tuning head**) is set apart from the body, with the **neck** connecting the two.

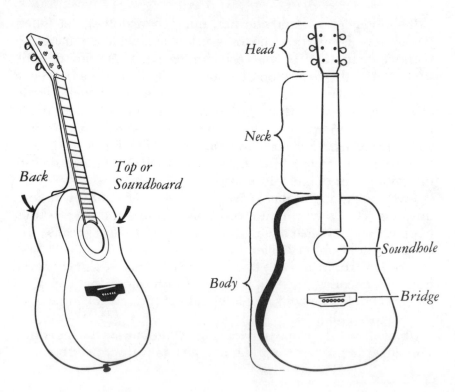

Back

Top or Soundboard

Head

Neck

Body

Soundhole

Bridge

Jazz guitars, Dobros and a few even more unusual designs do not have round **soundholes**, and owners of such exceptional instruments will please bear with me until I discuss variations on the basic classic or folk guitar design.

Acoustically, the most important part of a guitar is the **top**. That's the large, light-colored (unless stained) face of the guitar with the soundhole cut into it and the **bridge** glued to it. The top is also called the **soundboard**, because it is the board which amplifies and colors the sound. It acts like the paper cone of a speaker. With very few exceptions, the soundboard is made of spruce, while no other part of a guitar is made of spruce. "Why?," you might ask.

There are thousands of different kinds of trees, each producing its own type of wood with its own characteristics—hardness, color, coarseness of grain, flexibility, etc. Every tree can be classified as either **evergreen** (like a Christmas Tree) or **deciduous** (if it drops its leaves every winter). When a deciduous tree drops its leaves, it's growth slows down a lot and the fibers formed during this time get packed very tightly together. This makes the wood denser and harder than wood produced by evergreen trees, so lumberpersons refer to the wood of evergreens as **softwood** and the wood of deciduous trees as **hardwood**.

Spruce, a softwood, is uniquely strong for its weight. Other softwoods are too weak to hold up to the string tension for years without buckling. All hardwoods, on the other hand, are too heavy to vibrate easily enough to make a good soundboard. Except for the soundboard, every part of a guitar needs to be harder and stronger than spruce, so different hardwoods are chosen for these parts.

All this is to stress that the top of your guitar is different from any other part. It is soft. *Very soft*. Your fingernail is harder than spruce.

A SHORT STORY FROM THE VOICE OF EXPERIENCE

Once, while playing my first guitar, I started faking flamenco music with a friend on mandolin. It started getting hotter and flashier until the friend tore loose on a really hot riff. My response was to mindlessly pound out the rhythm on the top of the guitar.

Later I discovered lots of little puncture-like dents in the top of my guitar, shaped, surprisingly like the ends of my fingernails. All the regret in the world couldn't smooth over that mistake. Dented and gouged spruce does not heal.

Remember: No other part of a guitar is as soft and vulnerable as the top.

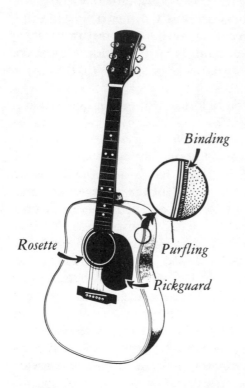

Now, you'll understand the necessity of a **pickguard** and **binding**. They protect the spruce from dings and gouges. If your guitar has steel strings, the manufacturer probably expects you to play it with a pick. (If you don't know what a pick is, your music store will be glad to sell you lots of them.) A pick. like your fingernail, is harder than spruce. Because strums often spill over the strings onto the top, you can think of a pickguard as a bib for guitarists. If your guitar uses nylon strings, it shouldn't have a pickguard, and without a pickguard, thou shalt not use a pick. NEVER! Not even if you promise to be *really* careful. NEVER!

Now look at the outside edge of your guitar. You'll see a stripe running all the way around. it is called the binding. On most guitars, the binding is a strip of plastic, though some handmade guitars use a strip of hardwood. Besides decoration, its function is to protect the edge of the spruce top. Without it, it would be very easy to chip the edge of the top. The binding also seals off the endgrain where wood otherwise breathes easily, rapidly changing its moisture content. So why stop that process? Because rapid change causes swelling and shrinking of pieces which can destroy a guitar.

A word on *moisture*: When a tree is alive, it is full of water, like all other living things. Chop it up into small pieces, and there's an exchange of moisture between the wood and the surrounding air. For a long time after it's cut, the wood has more water than the air, so as things get in balance, the wood dries. Some wood dealers allow this to happen at its natural pace in open air, producing what's called air-dried wood. Others speed up the process by heating the air in ovens called kilns. The hotter air is thirstier, sucking the moisture from the wood and causing it to dry faster. This process produces kiln-dried wood. It is debatable whether a kiln damages wood, making it significantly inferior to air-dried wood, but there *is* a physical difference. Air-dried wood is much more expensive.

Whatever way it's dried, once the wood moisture content matches the relative humidity of the air, the wood takes on or gives off moisture to match changes in the air's relative humidity. Humidity changes constantly and in heated and air-conditioned homes it can change faster than anywhere in nature.

The problem is that wood, like a sponge, changes size with changes in moisture. The individual fibers don't get any longer or shorter, but they do get fatter. Different parts of your guitar are glued together at different angles. Because these parts swell or shrink across their width and not along their length, pressure may be created as one piece wants to swell one way while it is glued to a piece which wants to well in a different direction. This stress changes the tone, and may even warp and split the various pieces of your instrument. Most likely of all to split is, of course, your top.

By sealing off the endgrain, the binding lessens the chance of splitting due to changes in the air's relative humidity. There's another strip of binding which protects the **back** as well. Most guitars also have contrasting colored stripes just inside the binding. This is mainly decorative and is called **purfling**.

Strips of purfling are also used for decoration around the soundhole. This decoration is called a **rosette**. Steel-stringed guitars usually use a few simple rings of black/white plastic (celluloid) purfling, while classic guitars traditionally have more complex decorations. A classic rosette is usually a mosaic design composed of tiny chips of contrasting wood (sometimes dyed to contrasting colors, or sometimes selected for naturally contrasting colors), forming a repeating pattern bordered by concentric rings of purfling.

Whichever rosette your guitar has, you should appreciate this beautiful little area on your guitar. Except for the CHEAPEST guitars, this is not a decal. A shallow groove is cut into the spruce top and the rosette or purfling is glued into the slot. Then it is scraped down until it is flush with the top. I don't care if it *is* often done completely by machine these days, I'm *still* impressed by this. Stare at it for a while, rub your fingers over it and enjoy it. It's one of those little joys that non-guitarists seldom experience.

> The name "rosette" harkens back to the days of olde when guitars and lutes (and any other stringed musical instrument with a round soundhole) had a sawn or carved grill-like decoration—called a *rose*—covering the soundhole. Why they called it a rose is as much your guess as mine. They did not, as one might expect, look like roses. Typically they were complex entanglements of geometric shapes or radiating patterns, like some sort of large, wooden snowflake. A rose might either have been cut out of the top, like a lot of little soundholes which together are pretty to look at; or it might have been a separate piece of sawn and carved wood; or even stiff, decorated paper, glued into place, filling a round soundhole.

For a variety of reasons, the rosette replaced the rose as a guitar soundhole decoration. For one, it's easier to make. It can be done with the tools and techniques already needed to build other parts of the guitar. Perhaps it also dampens the tone a tad less.

Like maps need designations such as North, South, East and West, the body needs terms to refer to its various areas. The **bass** and **treble** sides refer to the strings associated with those sides (the bass strings are the fat ones to your left when the guitar top is viewed as in the illustration, and the treble strings are the thinner ones to your right. The **upper bouts** (sometimes called **shoulders**), **waist**, and **lower bouts** refer to the areas defined by the curves of the profile.

The **bridge** is that dark, usually rectangular piece glued to the top, through which all vibrations must travel to get from a string to the soundboard. On most guitars, the strings are also anchored there.

The white tab which sticks up from the bridge—the strings lie across it—is called a **saddle**. I've tried to figure out how it got it's name, but the explanations get far out even for me. Though the saddle is obviously a separate piece from the bridge, the term bridge usually includes the saddle, like the term car includes tires.

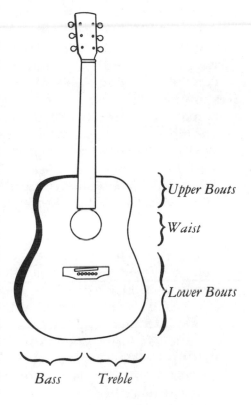

Upper Bouts

Waist

Lower Bouts

Bass   *Treble*

So what does a bridge *do*? Imagine yourself as a guitar string. Somebody plucked you and you're giving it all you've got. Problem is, nobody can hear you. You are vibrating your brains out, but you're so skinny you can't shove around enough air to get your message to the human ear. Hundreds of square inches of thin, resonant spruce lie less than an inch away, just waiting to broadcast your message to the world. You wiggle up and down,

TOP VIEW (Steel-String Bridge)

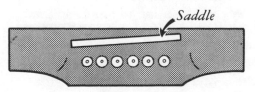

Saddle

SIDE VIEW (Classic Bridge)

Saddle

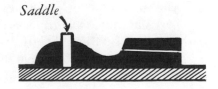

throwing your weight toward the top, then away from it, tugging at your anchoring point in pulses.

When you do that, you shove the saddle up and down and wiggle it back and forth. It must take all of this dancing without being heavy or spongey, which would absorb too much of the sound energy. It also must be hard and strong enough to avoid being cut by you. Traditional materials which satisfy these requirements are ivory and bone, though most modern guitars have saddles made of white plastic.

All this motion gets transferred to the bridge, which is usually rosewood or ebony, both very dense woods. Vibrations here tend to carry throughout the bridge, a relatively large and heavy moving object in the middle of a thin spruce membrane. In the same way that a speaker coil shoves the speaker cone in and out, the bridge shoves the soundboard in and out. Having the string ends tied or pegged at the bridge transfers even more of the sound energy to it. So that's how it's done.

In reality, it's more complex than this, but this should give you an idea of fundamental guitar acoustics.

Although the top does most of the vibrating, you should realize that the back affects the tone quite a bit, too. Since the top and back are both rather large, thin areas of wood, the qualities of the wood (density, flexibility, etc.) effect the sound *very* much.

A log may be cut all sorts of ways to make lumber. When you view the end of a log that's been cut, however, you'll notice that all of your splits and cracks go through the heart of the log. The relationship between the heart of the wood and the sides and edges of the board determines whether a board is slab-cut or quartersawn.

Splits and cracks are not desirable in guitar tops and backs. A slab-cut piece is quite prone to split, especially when it's as wide and thin as a guitar top or back. A quartersawn piece can split, but not nearly as easily as a slab-cut piece (as you'll find out if you try to split firewood along a line that does not go through the heart). Quartersawn wood also warps less and is strong and more springy than slab-cut. Take my word for it. People who work with wood have noticed this for centuries.

There's one problem with using quartersawn planks for soundboards: one edge is closer to the center of the tree than the other.

Trees, like people, grow faster when they are younger. Because the thickness of each *growth ring* represents one year's growth, and each year the tree builds a new layer around the outside, near the center the rings are generally farther apart than the rings near the outside of the tree (denser grained). But boards are inconsistent. Some have nearly equal grain along the entire width, while others are much closer grained on one side than the other.

Long ago some smart person figured it was better to be symmetrical than unpredictably natural. Since then, guitar tops and backs have been made out of *book matched sets*. That means that to make a top or back of a guitar you begin with a piece of wood half as wide and twice as thick as the panel you want to make. This piece is then cut edgewise to make two pieces half as thick. These two pieces are then opened up like the covers of a book and glued edge to edge. Ta da! Bookmatched!

For your appreciation, start counting the number of lines on your guitar top and realize that each one took a year to form. That tree was *old*. It took over a hundred years to make that piece of wood. Take good care of it.

The sides of a guitar are similarly cut from a single piece of wood. For solid wood guitars, this is necessary for acoustic reasons. For plywood guitars, it's done primarily to make them look more like solid wood guitars. The construction of plywood is such that the density of the finished product is a bit more consistant across the entire board than that of solid wood. Book matched veneers are prettier than mismatched sides, or one large, uneven panel of veneer.

You might enjoy looking at the joint running up the center of the top and back of your guitar. Often, it's not very easy to follow, but it's there.

If you intend to stand while playing your guitar, you'll need a **strap**. You'll also need something to attach the strap to. Fittingly, the area between the lower bouts of the guitar is called the **tail**. Although the sides are too thin to support any sort of peg or screw to hold a strap, right at the tail there's an internal block of wood called the **tail block**. A **tail pin** is plugged into a suitably shaped hole drilled through the outside of the guitar into this tail block. The tail pin is also referred to as an **end pin** or **strap button**.

Guitar straps come with a keyhole-shaped orifice at each end. One goes over the tailpin, while the other is usually attached in one of four ways to the neck end of the guitar. (See the insert illustrations.) Note that most steel stringed guitars come with tailpins, and most classic guitars don't. Classic guitarists *sit* while playing.

The **neck** is usually made of Honduras mahogany. It's a very plentiful wood which is very stable—it doesn't tend to warp—and it takes carving well without chipping. On nylon-stringed guitars, the neck takes the string tension all on its own. On steel stringed guitars, it has a steel **truss rod** inside the neck to help it take the tug without bowing or breaking.

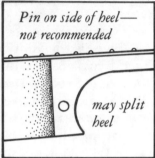

Pin on side of heel— not recommended

may split heel

The darker plank of wood glued to the top side of the neck which goes all the way to the soundhole is called the **fingerboard** or **fretboard**. The latter name comes because it is the board onto which are mounted all the **frets** (the little metal strips that form lumps in an otherwise smooth surface).

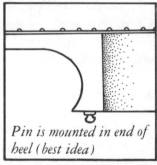

Pin is mounted in end of heel (best idea)

It may seem weird to locate a part named a **heel** on the backside of the neck (I suppose it could have been called a *nape*), but on a handmade classic guitar, the heel forms the back edge of a foot-shaped block of wood which is part of the neck, but *inside* the guitar soundbox. You can see it through the soundhole of a *handmade* classic guitar. Other guitars join the neck to the body with a different type

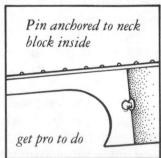

Pin anchored to neck block inside

get pro to do

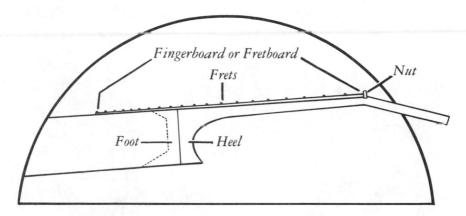

of joint, and all you'll see inside the guitar is a rectangular block. There is more about this in the Repair chapter.

The **nut** is that white piece with the slots in it at the end of the fingerboard. It is important because it holds the strings at the proper distance from each other and from the fingerboard. You'll become very familiar with this little chunk of bone, ivory or plastic as soon as you try your hand at adjusting your action. (It'll all make sense in time).

The assembly just above the nut is called the **tuning head**. There are three basic types. Steel-string guitars usually have **tuning buttons** which stick out of the sides of the head. These chunks of plastic, bone or ebony are mounted on what turns out to be axles for the **tuning gears**, which may or may not be enclosed by a metal box. Be they enclosed or not, the gears are normally mounted on a plate which is screwed to the backside of the tuning head.

Sometimes each tuning gear has its separate **mounting plate**, but often three **tuning machines** (that's the assembly composed of one tuning button, its corresponding roller, and all the machinery between) are ganged together on one mounting plate.

When you turn the buttons, the gears twist the **rollers** (sometimes called *spools*) to which the strings are anchored (they're sort of wrapped, and sort of tied). That's how you tighten and loosen the strings to tune them.

Classic guitars use almost the same mechanism, except the rollers are fatter. And instead of placing the mounting plate at the back of the head with the rollers going through holes in the back

FLAMENCO PEG HEAD

SLOTTED HEAD FOR CLASSIC GUITAR

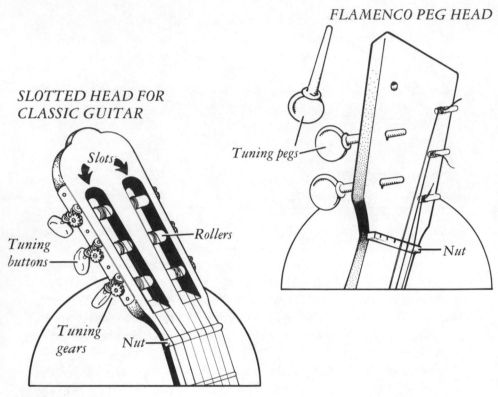

Slots

Rollers

Tuning buttons

Tuning gears

Nut

Tuning pegs

Nut

STEEL-STRING TUNING HEAD

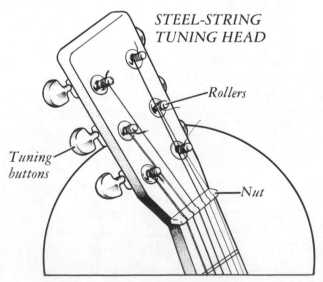

Rollers

Tuning buttons

Nut

of the head to protrude on the topside, the mounting plate is mounted on the *side* of the tuning head, so the rollers go inward through holes in the sides of the head. The slots give you access to the rollers.

There are also some rather exotic tuning machines which use ball bearings and such—someone will probably come up with a hydraulic set before long—but this sort of contraption is exceptional.

Flamenco guitars don't use any sort of metal tuning machine at all. Usually they just have straight, slightly conical wooden pegs sticking up through corresponding holes. They are wedged in place just tight enough not to slip and just loose enough not to bind when you turn them.

If you have a flamenco guitar (or any other instrument with pegs) and the pegs slip, push them in a little tighter. If that doesn't work, get some peg dope or blackboard chalk and rub it on the sides of the peg. If that doesn't work, you probably need to have the holes reamed or the pegs shaved to get them back into a round cross section. See a luthier. (Look in the yellow pages under "Musical Instruments—Repair" or find a violinist and ask to whom she or he goes.)

You should check how snugly pegs fit their holes any time an instrument goes through a change in humidity. In very rare, extreme cases, pegs can swell or holes can shrink enough to split the tuning head. More commonly, pegs stick, making it difficult to tune. Usually such a sticky peg may be freed by pulling and twisting it, then gently pressing it back into place. If it remains sticky, you might remove it and rub the sides of the peg with a bar of soap. If a peg sticks so badly that you can't budge it, tap it with a

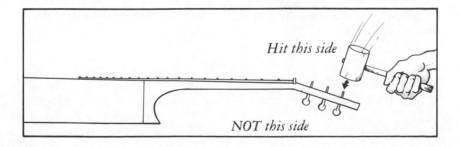

Hit this side

NOT this side

mallet to drive it out of its hole. (If you use a hammer you will probably dent the end of the peg.)

Even the strings have terms. The three fattest strings are called **bass strings** (pronounced like base and not like the fish) while the three skinniest ones are called **treble strings**. Notice that the fattest strings have thin wire wrapped around them. They are called **wound strings** (rhymes with pound and not with swooned).

Of interest to history buffs, stringmakers started winding thin wire around a core to make bass strings in the Late Renaissance/Early Baroque period (around 1600). For a long time prior to that they had known that a fatter, heavier string played a lower note than a thinner one of the same length and tension. The problem was that gut strings came only so fat, and thick metal wire acted a lot like the wire presently used to make clothes hangers; that is, not very musical. Winding a thin wire around the bass strings made them heavier without making them significantly stiffer.

That probably had a lot to do with the increased range of later instruments. They kept adding strings to get lower and lower notes on their lutes, guitars (originally with 4 pairs of strings), and harpsichords. Guitars stopped at our present low E, but lutes kept having strings added until only a dedicated maniac could play them. They became "less fashionable" (people threw them away). It is also noteworthy that paintings of lute players show them *tuning* more often than *playing*. Keyboard instruments kept adding bass strings until the piano got its present *ridiculously* low A at the bottom—unless you have a 9 foot grand piano, that note is impossible to tune. There's even one company which builds pianos with even *lower* notes. Their lust for lows verges on the subsonic.

Well, there's your tour. I hope that now you can look at a guitar and see more than a pile of pieces or a single blob. It might even be a little more interesting now. That was the goal, anyway. Enjoy.

CHAPTER 2

Choosing Your Instrument
(or understanding the one you've ended up with)

Maybe you're starting out with an instrument without having personally picked it out. It's a gift or maybe it was found in an attic, left behind by a roomate who skipped town without paying rent, or just dropped out of the sky into your arms. So now what do you do with it?

First, you need to figure out just what it was designed for. Different guitars need different things to become good instruments and life companions.

If you don't already have an instrument and you want to select one, you might be facing our old enemy—Ignorance. Don't fret. There are a lot of very different types of guitars to choose from, but you may learn enough in this chapter to choose the one that will suit you for years to come.

Kinds of Guitars, What They Need, and What They Do

THE BASIC STEEL-STRINGED FOLK GUITAR

You can distinguish this from other types of guitars by the pick guard, the tuning head with 6 tuning machines suited for steel strings, the flat top, pin bridge, and round soundhole. This guitar

INSIDE THE TOP

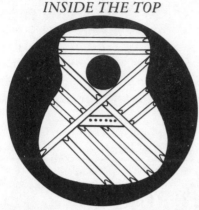

was designed primarily to accompany a singer, though folks have definitely developed techniques, like bluegrass flatpicking, for doing other things with it. It is the right instrument for you if you intend to strum chords and sing songs.

Compared to nylon-string guitars, the top is thick and a bit more heavily braced inside, typically in an "X" pattern. This enables it to stand the high tension of steel strings and to produce a very loud sound when played with a pick. Metal or plastic fingerpicks are often used. If you get a real honey of a steel-string folk guitar, such as a nice Martin with scalloped (see page 69) braces and light-gauge strings, you can also sound pretty good fingerpicking with your bare fingernails, but the average mass-produced folk guitar gets severe laryngitis without the power of a pick to get it started. Another common name for this type of instrument is the **flat-top acoustic** guitar, though to *really* specify this type of guitar, you need a ridiculously long name such as: flat-top acoustic six steel-string guitar, and there are still different types in *this* group!

THE 12-STRING GUITAR

Basically, it's the same as the folk guitar, except that every string is doubled. The bass pairs of strings are tuned in octaves—an octave is the musical distance between the two "do"s in "do, re, me, fa, sol, la, ti, do." The highest pitched pairs of strings are tuned to the same note because they are already very thin and high pitched. Strings that would go an octave higher would break too easily. This guitar gives a fuller, richer, more resonant sound when strumming chords. Followers of Leo Kottke do other things on a 12-string, but it's the tone color that makes it desirable over a normal 6-string folk guitar.

There's only one problem with a 12-string guitar: its got 12 strings. That means more tension on the guitar, so the neck tends to warp, the bridge tends to come off, and the top tends to buckle. Only wizards can tune them—you definitely should watch someone try to tune one before investing in one. The high D and G strings frequently break, and a set of strings is not cheap. Also realize that a cheap 12-string guitar is no bargain. Most have tuning machines that bring great pain to the left hand as you try to twist stiff tuners with miniature buttons.

I've seen two 12-string guitars I'd like to own. One went for about $3,200 and the other probably listed for about $1,200 before it had what should have been many hundreds of dollars of rebuilding by a phenomenal luthier. I sincerely suggest you try a 6-string first.

For those who are determined to be serious about the 12-string guitar I offer another problem and a solution. 6-string guitars have a bridge that is slanted so the bass strings are longer than the treble strings. This is necessary because when you fret a string, you stretch it and it goes sharp (the pitch goes higher), and heavier strings go sharper than thinner ones when stretched the same distance. So the bass strings need to be longer than the treble strings in order to play in tune.

A 12-string guitar has pairs of strings tuned an octave apart. If you tune the strings perfectly to the octave when playing the strings open, when you fret a pair of strings, the bass string goes sharper than its mate an octave higher. The only way around this is a **segmented saddle**. That means that each string gets its own saddle so the length is right for each string to play in tune.

Figuring out just what the right length really should be is a trick in itself. Jay Darmstadter has a system using a strobe tuner to precisely set the right length for any given guitar with any given brand of strings at any preferred height to the playing action. As of February 1982 he did it for about $100 (not bad for the difference it makes). Here's how to contact him: Jay's Place, 1724 Allied Street, Charlottesville, VA 22901. Tell him Will sent ya.

THE DOBRO

If you don't know what one is, you don't want one. And if you *do* want one, you don't need me to tell you why. It is an acoustic guitar with metal resonators built in. It is very loud and twangy

CLASSIC GUITAR

JAZZ GUITAR

12-STRING GUITAR

FLAMENCO GUITAR

DOBRO GUITAR

STEEL-STRING GUITAR

and is often played with a slide or bottleneck—a metal bar or a glass tube used to slide notes like a trombone instead of fretting fixed pitches—while the player lays it across his or her lap. For this purpose, the nut is usually very high so the slide can be used without striking the frets. To facilitate playing chords and thirds— a word that I hope will make sense before you finish the book— the dobro is commonly tuned differently than the most typical tuning for guitar.

Coffeehouse blues players also appreciate its twangy tones, though they usually hold it and tune it like folk guitars.

Country music groups are greatly enriched by a good dobro player, but it is pretty much a folksy learn-it-from-someone-who-already-plays-it traditional instrument. I don't play one, so if you are really interested in dobros, you'll have to ask a dobro player.

THE ARCH-TOP GUITAR, "F"-HOLE GUITAR, OR JAZZ GUITAR

Well, it has an arched top instead of a flat top, "f" holes like a fiddle instead of a round soundhole, and it's used primarily for jazz. The fiddle-like top is much stiffer than a flat top, killing any long resonances that a folk guitar might promote. Jazz players don't want long resonance; they want short, stinging notes for amazingly fast scale runs and riffs.

Note that like a fiddle, this guitar anchors the strings to a tailpiece. Also like a fiddle, it uses a movable bridge. This means that the bridge is not glued to the top. It is held in place by the string tension alone and if you remove all the strings at once while changing strings, the bridge will fall off, and you'll have to figure out exactly where to put it. I'll cover that in the tuning chapter.

THE CLASSIC GUITAR

Unlike all of the guitars discussed to now, this instrument uses nylon treble strings and bass strings of stranded nylon wrapped with metal. Also, it has no pick guard, for the design of this instrument predates the use of picks for guitars.

Originally, all guitars had *gut* strings. Some people call it *cat gut*, but it's usually sheep intestines (if you find a cat as big as a sheep, you usually don't want to mess with it) which have been cleaned out, stretched, twisted and dried. During the later 1800s, C. F.

Martin and a few others decided that steel strings could be used as well. So they built guitars suited to the higher tension and developed the newer folk guitar design. Meanwhile, the older design also changed a bit, getting larger while experimenting with newer bracing designs, but still using gut strings and being played with a nude right hand. Du Pont came up with nylon to replace the gut—to the relief of a lot of sheep—but the basic design is still pretty much the same as it was in the mid-1800s, so it's referred to as the *classic* (or *classical*) guitar.

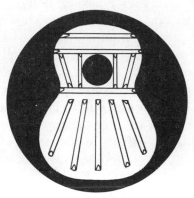

TRADITIONAL FAN BRACING
(inside classic guitar)

Do not put steel strings on a classic guitar. It will sound great for a while if you do. I've heard two such guitars. Both were very loud and resonant. I talked one owner into changing back to nylon strings. The other owner's instrument quickly developed a warped neck, buckling top and separating bridge. It became not only impossible to play, but *ugly*.

Do not use a pick on a classic guitar. NEVER!!! There is no pick guard, and the instrument should be sensitive enough to make lots of sound *without* a pick.

Classic guitars are used primarily for solo classical music. It is a chamber instrument, occasionally used in orchestras or with small instrumental ensembles, though sometimes it is used in more folky settings, fingerpicking chords to accompany a song. If you want to play like Segovia, Julian Bream, John Williams or Christopher Parkenning, you want a classic guitar. If you want to strum chords or play bluegrass, you probably want something else.

THE FLAMENCO GUITAR

Like a dobro, if you don't know what it is, you don't want one. It is a very traditional variation on the classic guitar design. The body is not as deep, and the traditional selection of wood for the

31

back and sides is different. It usually uses tuning pegs instead of a slotted head with tuning machines, and it usually has clear plastic pick guards called *golpeadors* ("golper" is Spanish for "to hit") on both sides of the top next to the strings. Golpeadors exist because flamenco players pound the hell out of the tops of their guitars with fingernails, knuckles, palms, and thumbs while frailing out the hottest flash of any form of guitar playing (the Spanish root of the word flamenco means *flaming*). A flamenco player doesn't want you to be emotionally moved, hum along, tap your foot, or in any way appreciate the music without thinking of the player. He or she wants you to sit in awe and be dumbfounded. If you like Houdini, Paganini, P. T. Barnum, Kiss and Evil Kneaval, you'd probably love flamenco. My love for flamenco died when I found little holes in the top of my guitar. . . .

BRIEFLY, OTHER TYPES

There are acoustic bass guitars, usually fat and colorful, with 4 gut strings tuned an octave below the four lowest strings of a normal guitar. Then there are tenor guitars which have only the top 4 strings of a regular guitar. Nine-string folk guitars double the 3 bass strings but leave the trebles single, as a compromise between 6 and 12 strings. During the 1800s and early 1900s, harp-guitars were built with the regular 6 strings plus an entire harp of bass strings that were played with the thumb without any attempt to fret those strings with the left hand. There's at least one 10-stringed variation on the classic guitar using the same principle of additional bass strings.

It goes on forever. I even saw an ad for a double necked acoustic guitar—one 6-string neck, and one 12-string neck, coming out at a slight angle from an 18-string bridge. This does not strike me as a good idea considering the tension problems of a mere 12-string, plus having one set of strings resonating aimlessly while you play on the other neck.

I gave up trying to keep track of it all when I saw a picture of Arlo Guthrie playing an electric 12-string dobro. If you are really gadget hungry and want to be different, go ahead and dig into one of these contraptions; but if you want to learn to play guitar, you'd best start with something more basic.

Brand Names

If you've got lots of friends with guitars, you've probably decided already what you like. It's primarily a matter of personal taste. I have friends who swear by Gibsons and think Martin has the wrong idea about how to make a guitar. Meanwhile, I'd use most Gibsons I've seen for dart boards, and I've played Martins for which I've developed sincere and profound lust.

One friend grabbed my arm when he found out I was writing this book and said, "Make sure to say something good about Yamaha. They make some really nice guitars for incredibly cheap prices."

Another friend fired back, "Yeah, but that was before Sigma flooded the market with really fine, affordable guitars." I was amazed. These guys are normal people, and suddenly they sound like TV commercials. The simple fact is, competition is tight in this field, and even if there were a perfect company from which to buy the perfect guitar, that might change by the time you read this book.

One word of caution: Ovation guitars are designed primarily for the stage where they will be electronically amplified. Their piezo-electric pickups have a distinctive sound, and their plastic bodies are immune to the sudden changes in heat and humidity caused by stage lighting. They are pretty and flashy, and they've got really nice tuning machines, but for the down-home-pull-it-out-from-under-the-bed-and-mess-around player or the acoustically-jam-with-friends picker, you can spend a lot less for a much better sounding acoustic guitar.

Of course, if it's worth a few hundred extra dollars to play the same model guitar as Glen Campbell, go ahead. Pleasure is the reason you're buying a guitar, right? But don't be surprised if some of your friends politely refuse your offer to strum a few tunes on your new Ovation. Some guitarists are allergic to plastic. They hug *wood*.

I personally would love to have an Ovation in addition to my wooden guitars. Then I could play in the rain and fight off muggers. Also, if I were ever on a sinking ship, I'd have my own personal liferaft.

Generally, there is as much variation among individual guitars of the same brand and model as between two different brands or models. I love Martin guitars—by coincidence they carry my name. Someday I might find one I don't like. Someday I might be able to afford one—Will Martin *will* own a *Martin* someday.

One word of advice to Martin owners: If you go to festivals or other public gatherings with your guitar, buy a second case—a plain black one. Those pretty blue or black hard shell cases with **MARTIN** written on them also have **STEAL ME FIRST** written all

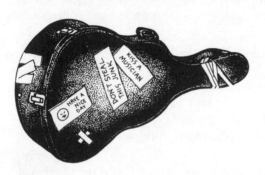

over them. Put bumper stickers all over your plain case and throw it down a stairwell a few times— without the guitar in it. Strips of masking tape are a nice addition. Make it look like something *no-body* would steal. When you open it in front of un-suspecting, appreciative eyes, listen for the excited gasp and the meek, trembling, "C-c-can I touch it?" Then you can bargain for special favors.

Use your **MARTIN** case only after you've at least reached brown belt ranking in karate, are carrying a gun, or are accompanied by a bodyguard whom you trust profoundly.

Beyond brand names, you really should try out the particular guitar you are going to buy *before* you buy it. Better yet, bring a friend who plays *better* than you. Let them try it out while you listen to both the guitar and the friend. Don't listen to the salespeople. They're getting paid for selling guitars. If they've got a limited stock of really good guitars and some that are bad enough to be difficult to unload, which do you think they'll try to sell you?

Handmade Guitars

If you really want a nice guitar, buy one made by human hands. If you are ready for a human built guitar, you probably know this already. Meanwhile, if you ask someone what kind of guitar they've got and they sneer at the suggestion that you are asking for a brand name, they probably have a good reason for sneering. Handmade instruments are a whole different creature. They sound a lot better and play a lot easier than anything made on an assembly line. You'll get more kinds of sound from such an instrument. The main reason I like Martins is that their building techniques approach the quality of handmade instruments more closely than other mass-produced guitars. In fact, some hand builders can't match Martin's quality. That's why they're so expensive.

In this field, you buy by builder name instead of brand name. It's best to look at other instruments the builder has made and/or to test the instrument itself before you buy it. A good guitar usually is made of well over $100 in materials, plus anywhere from two weeks to a few months of an experienced builder's undivided attention using specialized tools in a controlled environment. If they sell it for under $1,000 they're fools.

Cases

A softshell case is fine if you never intend to take the instrument out of your room. Otherwise, a hardshell case is worth the investment if you've got any value at all in the guitar.

You know that little key they give you to lock your case? Throw it away. Anybody who would steal your guitar will steal the case and break the lock. The lock is good only against toddlers who are old enough to open regular latches, but not inventive enough *yet* to use a fingernail file.

Cases with locks are like driveways with **Private—Keep Out** signs. If you didn't intend to trespass, you wouldn't need to see the sign. If you did intend to trespass, the sign wouldn't stop you.

Features to Avoid in Selecting a Guitar

An *adjustable bridge* is a bad idea on an acoustic guitar. Any guitar bridge can be adjusted with a file or some shims, but when

Normal Classic Bridge

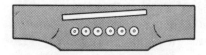

Normal Steel-String Bridge

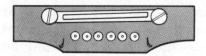

Adjustable Steel-String Bridge (not good)

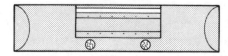

Cheap Classic Bridge

a salesperson talks about an adjustable bridge they are referring to a bridge with a metal base where the height is adjusted by two metal screws. You don't need any metal in your guitar, except in or on the neck and the tuning head, which don't have to conduct sound.

Metal is *heavy*. In orchestras, when the violins want to mute their tone, they stick a piece of metal on their bridges. That's what adjustable bridges do for you. They mute the tone by adding unneeded weight to the bridge.

They also distort the tone. Instead of each string separately delivering sound to the wooden top, the adjustable bridge is jacked up on the two adjustment screws. Bass tones just can't make the trip; they stay right there on the string and only a whisperred echo of a note ever makes it to the guitar top. You get a dull, thuddy bass and a distorted treble. In case you haven't noticed, I do not favor adjustable bridges.

The same goes for mother-of-pearl dots on the bridge. They are usually plastic imitation mother-of-pearl, and they cover metal screws that were used to hold the bridge on. If the guitar is built with any care, you won't need any screws to hold the bridge on. Like an adjustable bridge, the screws mute the tone.

A *zero fret* is a bad idea on any guitar.

This was the creation of an engineer who wanted a really cheap way to guarantee good alignment between the fret spacing and the nut. If you are mass producing millions of guitars with zero quality control, a zero fret becomes a good idea. It slightly affects how easily the string slips through a nut while tuning, sort of like tuning with your capo on.

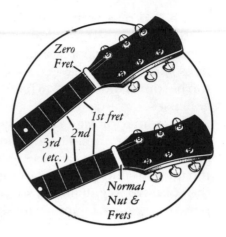

A **capo** is a device which holds a padded bar against all 6 strings at any given fret to raise the pitch of the guitar accompaniment to suit a voice which can't sing low enough for the guitar without a capo. Tuning with the capo on is like watering the lawn with your kid brother standing on the hose. From my perspective a zero fret is an indicator that the designer of the guitar put more emphasis on production techniques for his assembly line than on the quality of the finished product.

If you see a guitar with a neck that goes straight into the body without the normal tapered heel, take time out to read the neck repairs section concerning *other neck joints*; and look for a better guitar.

If you are buying a flat top acoustic guitar with a tailpiece, forget this

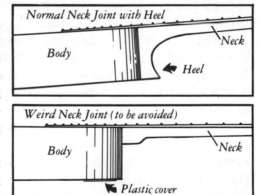

book. Such guitars are usually available only at discount department stores and are generally a waste of good plywood.

Laminates

I've been told that any guitar now costing less than $300 is made of *laminated wood*—salespeople avoid the word *plywood* like the plague. Aesthetically, plywood is the pits, but as far as the real world goes, it has both good and bad characteristics.

The bad part is that plywood is stiffer than solid wood, so it tends not to carry bass tones very well. Also, it doesn't fatigue and become more responsive to musical tones the way solid wood does after years of playing. Solid wood keeps improving until the top becomes too flexible to handle the string tension and it slowly collapses.

The primary advantages of plywood are durability, insensitivity to changes in humidity, and consistency. Ten million plywood guitars coming off of an assembly line will sound more alike than ten million solid wood guitars off the same assembly line. Many of the solid wood guitars will sound worse than the majority of the plywood guitars, so among mass-produced guitars it makes good sense to shift to plywood.

Plywood also never cracks, because the different layers of veneer—thin sheets of wood—have grains that are perpendicular to one another. Unlike solid wood it doesn't swell and shrink with humidity changes. Also, because it is made of veneers, you can make plywood out of logs that would not be of sufficient size and quality for solid lumber.

If you ever expect your instrument to handle exposure to extremes of heat, cold, humidity or dryness, a plywood instrument makes a lot of sense. Many of them even sound pretty nice. And the veneers may actually look better than what can be easily found in solid lumber.

Also, of course, the more plywood guitars that come off assembly lines, the more really nice wood there is left for builders who will individually adjust the thickness and brace the wood of a guitar to suit the best potential for that particular set of wood. An assembly line cannot take into consideration variations in grain, density and flexibility, and good wood alone cannot make a good guitar because wood is a very inconsistent material.

The best guitars are made of solid wood. They also are built by hand. If you can't afford (or don't choose to pay for) a hand-built instrument, you'd aid our ecology by accepting a plywood guitar. You'd also spare yourself the extra trouble of caring for a solid wood instrument, since solid wood is much more fragile.

Where To Look?

If you know you want a new guitar, take a guitar-playing friend with you and check out *several* stores. That will give you a wider selection and a good idea of what you can get for the money you intend to spend. If you are dazed and don't know how much you are willing to spend, having different priced guitars in your hands will help. You'll find guitars you'd hate at any price, and ones you'd love, but could never afford. If you've got enough money that you never experience this second condition, I know a starving author I'd like you to meet....

If fresh polish and newness isn't all that important to you, ask around the family (you'd be surprised who has a guitar stowed away that they never got around to using), look in the want ads, and check out local buy/sell trading post type publications. Again, take along a guitar-playing friend, unless you know enough or you've got enough money to buy a mistake.

Read the next section *before* you have a prospective guitar in your hands.

THE TEST RIDE

If you have decided on a classic guitar, you must pay particular and immediate attention to the neck. It is not adjustable. If it isn't right, it won't get better. Steel-string guitar buyers should also check out the neck, but shouldn't immediately dismiss a guitar that might just need adjustment. Here's how to check it:

With your left index finger, fret a string at the first fret, as if you were going to play that note. With your right index finger,

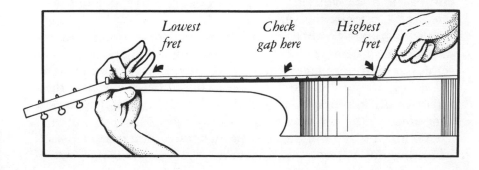

Lowest fret   Check gap here   Highest fret

fret the same string at the highest fret (right at the sound box end of the fingerboard). Now, using the string as a straight edge, sight down the edge of the fingerboard. Note particularly whether or not the string touches the frets in the middle. If it doesn't touch, how large is the gap? Ideally, the neck should be *very slightly . . .* **very** slightly warped so that the strings **almost** touch the frets in the middle.

If the gap is too great, it becomes impossible to play in upper positions—nearer the soundhole. If you ever intend to play more than simple chords, you'll eventually want to use those high frets too. It would be nice to be able to do so without having to buy another guitar.

If it's flat, the very slightest irregularity in fret height will be a substantial problem. Even if the frets are even now, they won't be after a few years of playing. Variations in humidity, combined with the human tendency to play some notes more often than others and to grip the neck like a vise, eventually create uneven frets.

If the neck is warped the other way, so that the strings touch in the *middle* first, forget the guitar. At best, you've got a nice wall hanging or a decorative planter, unless the neck is adjustable.

Check every string. It is quite possible to have a twist in the neck allowing the straightness to be different for each string. Even if your guitar has an adjustable neck, it won't adjust to correct this sort of twist.

You may be asking, "How can you tell if a guitar has an adjustable neck?" Adjustable truss rods stick out one end or the other of the neck. If it comes out at the tuning head, you can see a plastic cover between the nut and the spools. If it comes out at the body end of the neck, you can find it by looking into the soundhole toward the neck (see illustration).

Martin guitars do not have adjustable truss rods (though Sigma, the *Japanese Martin* does). They use hollow square tubes to reinforce their necks. They believe that it's strong enough to take the string tension, it doesn't *need* to be adjusted because they build it right the first time, and it doesn't change all that much over time.

One luthier friend thinks Martin has the wrong idea, and says he always finds Martins with *horrible* playing action. Meanwhile,

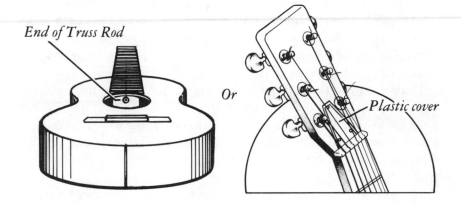

End of Truss Rod

Or

Plastic cover

I *love* the feel of every Martin I've ever played, and I played a guitar built by the luthier in question, and his neck was FLAT. It was as perfectly flat as I've ever seen on *any* guitar. It felt great. Only problem is that when any fret eventually sinks or rises just a little, he'll have to work over the entire fingerboard with a sharpening stone and a fret file. For a luthier, that's fine, but most of the rest of us would be a bit reluctant to dig into that sort of adjustment.

If the guitar you've got is a used one, check for fret wear. If there's a little dent on the fret under each string, it probably needs new frets. That's not usually an owner repair. It's best to get a luthier to do it. It costs money and often requires a lengthy separation from the instrument. Repairpersons and luthiers tend to shelve such a task, meditate on it, and wait for an inspiration to strike before they pick up your instrument to fix it. And *don't bug* a luthier. If he's got your guitar and hasn't fixed it yet and you rush him, you'll get it back fixed by a person who was pissed. That's bad Karma.

Also, check for wear in general. Most scratches, gouges, and even cracks are cosmetic and don't affect the tone. Some Old Timers even cherish a guitar that looks like it was in a cat fight and lost. That nice rainbow-shaped trough that extends beyond the pickguard is aesthetically appealing to them. Sweat stains, carved initials, and obvious home repairs are special signs of love and long-term devotion.

Other people faint at the thought of a scratch on the back side of the neck where nobody will ever see it. You'd best decide to which group you belong, or where you fit between. This instrument is possibly going to be your friend for a long time. Do the cosmetics really bother you?

Here's a good time to pause again to think about the urge you have to own a guitar. Close your eyes. Think guitar. What do you see? Do you see the guitar itself, or do you see yourself playing a guitar? Do you imagine playing for yourself, for a special friend, or for a crowd? Do you have a group of musicians you intend to play with?

If you want to play with others, conformity is something you shouldn't ignore. A starburst finish might not be welcome in an old-time musician's group. A well-worn, obscure brandname instrument might not fit a fashion conscious group of adolescent folk songsters.

If you want to play *for* others, pay attention to the image you are projecting. Does the guitar have sparkle and flash, or does it look warm and friendly? Does it suit your clothes?

If at the beginning of this exercise you saw the guitar all by itself, face it, you're in love. You don't care what anybody else thinks about how it looks. You've just got to have *that* guitar. Before you let appearances get you too carried away, you should continue your inspection to make sure you've chosen a guitar which will last.

If you see a crack, make sure it is only cosmetic. Tap all around it. (NOT with your fingernails. Murder, as a crime of passion, may be committed upon you by the prospective seller if you use anything harder or more abrasive than the fleshy part of your thumb.) Listen for buzzes or any indication of something loose inside. When you (or friend) play it, listen for any peculiar noises. Listen *hard*! Aside from making weird sounds, loose braces inside reduce the strength of the top against the string tension, resulting in a dead guitar without much time to get to know it.

If you are buying a new guitar, do this same check. Tap it all over the body just to make sure it's all glued up tight. I repaired a guitar once which was fairly new. The strings were off and while inspecting the insides, a brace came off in my hand. They don't build them like they used to. It was that sort of quality construction that had me repairing a new guitar in the first place.

Check where the body joins the neck. No new guitar should have a joint that doesn't look new and perfect. Used guitars sometimes have a little cosmetic split here. If that's the case with the guitar you're inspecting, warn the seller about what you are going to do, and if she or he's not willing to allow you to continue, realize the guitar *may* be trash. If you get the go-ahead, grip the neck in one hand, the body in the other near the tailpin, and press the neck joint of the guitar against your chest. Persons with large breasts may choose to kneel and press the guitar against a knee. Make the pressure slow, on and off, and never *too* much. You are trying to counterbalance the string tension, not break the guitar.

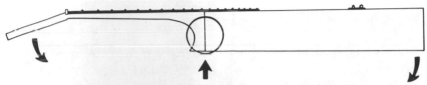

Arrows show slight pressure with 2 hands and chest or knee.
Circle shows where to watch.

Watch for any motion in the crack and listen for anything resembling a crunching, grating sound. If you hear such sounds, the neck joint is not sound . . . shesagonnabreak. Suggest to the owner that he or she quickly reduce the tension of the strings, lest he or she comes to own two pieces of what used to be one guitar. Refer them to the section on repairs for neck joints. If it appears to have broken on you, either it was already broken or was about to go anyway. Of course, the owner might have trouble seeing it that way.

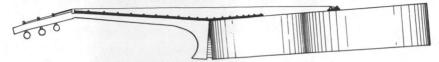

What's wrong with this guitar?

If the guitar is *inexpensive*, check the action height. This is the distance between the strings and the 12th fret when no strings are fretted. This can be adjusted to a certain degree on all guitars, but some guitars are just too far off for adjustment.

What is too far off? That varies from one guitar to another, and from one person to another. It should be high enough for you to play as loud as you're ever going to want to play without buzzing on the frets, and ideally, no higher. 1/2 inch is too high for a classic guitar. 3/8 inch is too high for a steel-string. If you can't bring it in any closer than that, the guitar is doomed to simple chords or you are doomed to painful left fingertips.

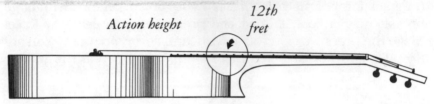

Action height   *12th fret*

Now, listen for tone. In purchasing a guitar you are basically buying a singing voice. Do you really want to sound like that? Also, realize that if you don't already play guitar, it's going to take a while to learn how to sound like anything at all. That's why you bring a friend.

That's about as much as a book can help you in picking out a guitar. It's all a matter of values. What do you like more: Guitar A, Guitar B, or the money? If you buy a guitar that's too cheap, it will be too difficult to play and you'll likely get discouraged and give up. If you buy too good of a guitar, because you aren't used to taking care of one yet you'll probably damage it before you get good enough to really appreciate it. But then, all important decisions are made on the basis of insufficient data. Good luck. Welcome aboard.

CHAPTER 3

Preservation & Maintenance

Preserving Your Instrument Through Proper Care

The man who built my guitar tells me that, of all the questions people ask at his shop, the majority have to do with how to care for an instrument. Few things teach us about mortality better than a broken guitar. We can help put off this lesson for a long time by some good judgment and the expenditure of minimal time and effort.

First, realize that there is a tremendous difference between the needs of a plywood guitar and one made of solid pieces. Plywood guitars primarily ask that you do not scratch, crush or burn them, and that you do little caring things for the shiny finish. Solid guitars threaten to crack on you if you, just once, put them through a climate change they don't like. That doesn't necessarily mean a winter trip from Florida to Nebraska. It may mean only the furnace coming on without any form or humidification.

Think of solid wood as hair held together by a clear, flexible glue which is by no means water repellant. These hairs fatten when moistened and get thinner when they dry out. A change in moisture content changes a board's thickness and width, though the length remains the same. The change in thickness is negligible in guitar wood because the wood is so thin. Meanwhile, before it's glued into place, a solid top for a guitar may change width by over 1/8" in a few hours if it is put through a major shift in humidity.

Why does it change thickness less than width? Each fiber swells or shrinks nearly equally in every direction along its thickness. Since the board is maybe 3/32" thick in some cases, that means dozens of wood fibers, each swelling or shrinking a small amount, so the thickness change is dozens of times the amount each fiber changes. But the width of the board is well over 12 inches, so you've got *thousands* of fibers along the width of the board each swelling or shrinking. The resulting change in the width of the board is thousands of times the change in thickness of each fiber.

In Colonial Williamsburg, Virginia, there is an instrument maker's shop built, of all places, over a stream. In the summer, the sun

shines on that stream and the humidity gets so high you can almost see a mist. They have the place sealed off as best they can, and there's an air conditioner/dehumidifier chugging its little heart out silently in the basement, 24 hours each day of warm, humid weather.

One time, the system died after everyone went home for the evening. Marcus, the father of my guitar, returned the next day to find an instrument he had been building in pieces, as if someone had placed a bomb in it. It literally had exploded.

Imagine the horror of being that instrument. It's late, and no one is around. Slowly, the air about you changes from a pleasant, cool crispness, to a stifling, muggy pressure. You feel yourself swelling and all of your joints ache from the stress. The pain mounts until finally, all of your pieces seek liberation in an explosion which cancels your existence.

Calm down. That's not likely to happen to a finished guitar under normal circumstances. That exploding instrument was *in the white*, which means Marcus hadn't put on any finish (that shiny stuff), and naked wood takes on moisture much faster than it does once the grain is sealed.

It is, however, not impossible. Generally, guitars are not sealed in any way on the inside. That means that air which goes into the soundhole meets raw wood. Some experiments have been made at finishing the inside of guitars, but that apparently has a detrimental effect on the tone, especially in the way the instrument mellows out with a few years' playing.

Guitars often explode, not unlike Marcus', in cargo compartments of planes and ships. In a plane, the cargo compartment is not pressurized as is the cabin, and the freezing temperatures and low air pressure at 30,000 feet or so above sea level is not a friendly environment for a guitar. If you travel by air with a guitar, either keep it with you, or get an air-tight case. One friend has her guitar stowed up front with the pilot when she flies, but those of us with less pulchritude might have a little more trouble mustering that much political clout.

The opposite problem occurs on ships. The high humidity can either burst the guitar, or the guitar might acclimate successfully (have all the parts shift around without damage) to the boat, and then split into pieces on shore as the wood dries and shrinks.

Cases do exist which protect instruments from this. They're usually handmade, very expensive, weigh a ton, and have a single rubber seal around the lid. They suck air like tupperware when you open or close them. They are worth their weight in gold.

There are even humidity hazards for your instrument in your own home. Think about what direct sunlight shining on a black guitar case does to the instrument inside. A hint: black is the color used in solar collectors to convert light into heat. Your guitar case becomes a portable, miniature solar kiln. That means hot and *dry*. Not good.

It's also not a good idea to spend a lot of time exposing a solid guitar to any sort of breeze. Moving air is often *changing* air, and it's fast change you want to avoid more than anything else. If you like playing outside, get a plywood guitar or expect to buy a new guitar often.

If your floor or walls are chilled in winter, it is better to have the case leaning against a wall with minimal surface contact, instead of lying flat on the floor. If you have a choice of leaning the case against an outside wall or one that divides your room from another room, the inside wall is the better choice. Even better, you might keep it in bed with you under cover. That's especially good if you are going through a time when nobody loves you more than your guitar.

Above all, avoid leaving it in the proximity of radiators, stoves, fireplaces, or heating/air conditioning ducts. These things violently change the heat and humidity of the air near them.

A Note of Reassurance: It has been pointed out to me that at this point many of you might get nightmares filled with exploding guitars and decide to take up the trumpet instead. First, let me remind you that it is difficult to sing and play trumpet at the same time, and kissing destroys your embouchure (the thing that trumpeters do with their lips to play trumpet) which is not a problem for guitarists.

Most guitars *never* explode. Plywood guitars are especially difficult to hurt. I never meant to say that guitars are easy to break. My point is that a guitar only has to break *once* to be broken. If you take care of it, it can last for many years. But you have to know what to avoid in order to know what taking good care of a guitar really means.

By now, you should be forming your own standards for how to keep an instrument. Having it *in* the case with the lid closed and latched whenever you aren't playing it is an excellent idea. More than anything else, the case is an insulator, protecting the instrument from sudden change. Even if your instrument is plywood, it is better to treat it in this manner, though it is not nearly as crucial.

The next consideration is that "I can see myself" shine. All guitars have some sort of finish to seal out drastic changes in humidity and prevent soil and human secretions from soaking into the wood, staining those luscious colors. The most common finish used today is spray lacquer or polyester. It is *very hard* and protective and seals out moisture well. It may be tinted from quite clear to downright opaque, with any desirable shade in between. It is applied with a spray gun or air brush and dries quickly, so it is ideally suited to mass production.

It's also better suited for plywood than solid wood, because along with being hard it is also *brittle*. Solid wood swells and shrinks, and the lacquer doesn't. That's the rub. After a couple of years the finish cracks up, looking like spider web patterns or a miniature model of a dried mudpuddle. Even on plywood, where cracking and crazing is not so much a problem, this stiff finish stiffens the wood and muffles the tone.

The only care this finish requires is an occasional wiping off with a soft damp cloth. If there's a spot which won't wipe off, you may *carefully* scrape it off with your fingernail because the finish is hard enough not to be easily scratched by something as soft as a fingernail (but remember, the spruce *under* the finish is *softer* than your fingernail).

On handmade guitars shellac is often used in a few coats, sanded between coats to provide a very *thin* protective finish that's less likely to dampen the tone of the instrument. Shellac is better able to stretch and shrink with the wood than the thicker spray lacquer, but it is still brittle by nature. It can crack and craze on a solid wood guitar, especially if applied too thickly or if the guitar weathers extremes in humidity. If it is too thin, it provides too little protection from moisture and crud.

If your guitar is handmade and you know it has been shellacked, wipe it often with a soft, damp cloth, but take care to avoid holding the cloth in one spot or dripping water droplets onto the finish. It may be so thin that it doesn't protect the wood extremely well from water, and more important, shellac turns white when you leave water on it. It is particularly bad about "water spotting."

Insofar as flexibility is concerned, an oil varnish is better than either of these finishes. This is the same sort of stuff Stradavarius used on his violins. It *never* cracks or crazes. What's the catch?

It is soft; *very* soft. It scratches very easily, and is not as complete a sealant as either shellac or lacquer. My classic guitar has such a finish. If I wear bluejeans and play that guitar, it picks up the fabric pattern where it touches my legs. When I pull it out of the case, I see that it has picked up the impression of the fuzz of the case lining wherever it touched the inside of the case. It is a hassle to care for, but I believe it contributes to the *wonderful* tone, and, like a dent in the surface of honey, minor scratches heal.

You might have noticed that, by my descriptions, there is no ideal guitar finish. That's simply because there isn't one. Each has its advantages and disadvantages. Technology has yet to invent a substance which can be applied to a guitar quickly and easily, which dries quickly to a really flexible, yet scratch resistant, waterproof, pretty coating which doesn't harm the acoustic properties of wood. Until such a product comes along, the makers of guitars choose among these partially successful finishes.

Waxes and polishes are not really good for guitars. Wax is something you add to the finish, making it a little thicker and heavier. Not good. It's also difficult to get off once it's on, and if you ever try to do a touchup on the finish, the new finish won't stick to the wax.

A polish is an abrasive. It smooths out the surface of a guitar finish by wearing away any protrusions, along with a certain amount of the smooth finish. On rare occasions it's okay to polish a guitar to get rid of fine scratches and bring back the luster, but the folks who sell the stuff would have you wipe it down with polish every time you pull it out of the case. From my perspective that's killing it with kindness.

A damp, soft cloth is all you need. The dampness loosens crud which is stuck to the guitar, and softens dust so you don't rake it across the guitar like sandpaper.

The main advice for care of any guitar finish is simply: *Be Careful*. Don't touch the surface with anything hard, sharp or abrasive. Don't wear a hazardous belt buckle, unless you either cover it with thick, soft cloth, or get used to the idea of owning a guitar with a gouged up back. Don't prop up your guitar in a chair or on the floor, or lean it against a chair, table or wall. The tuning head is the *heavy* end of the guitar, so propping it up is creating a situation where it can fall down. This often breaks the head joint or the neck joint, or bends the shafts of the tuning machines. Don't lay it down on the couch so someone entering the room to watch T.V., read, or daydream can sit on it.

The *only* intelligent way to treat your guitar is to keep it in the case when you aren't using it. Put the case next to where you intend to play the guitar, and if you put the guitar down for any reason, no matter how brief your intent (people get distracted and a moment becomes a weekend), put it back into the case, close the lid, and latch at least one latch. If this becomes an automatic habit, you can save yourself a *lot* of grief.

If you own a solid wood guitar that you will be keeping in a dry place (like a heated home in winter), go to the music store and buy a "Damp-it" for your guitar. That's a sponge, stuffed inside a perforated length of surgical rubber hose, with a clip for your soundhole. Follow directions to dampen the sponge, and keep it moist all the time when the weather is dry. This saves you from the horrors of a guitar which commits hari-kari, from minor cracks around the edges to a long, vented opening in the top or back.

The last word on care is that you should not allow a problem to creep up on you. Recently, at a music workshop, a fellow had a guitar with a bridge hanging on by a thin strip of glue along the front edge. His comment was "It's been rising up like this for some time now, but I never noticed that it was this *bad*. I guess I ought to get it fixed." He probably won't do so until it falls off.

The solution is to stop every now and then and take the time to look at your guitar as if you'd never seen it before. Wipe off all the dust, beerstains, dried up chewing tobacco or bubble gum. Look carefully at all cracks or separated joints and decide *early* what to do about them. Then *do* it. The worse it gets, the harder it is to fix.

CHAPTER 4

Tuning

Before you can play a guitar or even really check one out to adjust the action, you have to be able to tune one. It's important. Now that you are committed to being a guitar player, you will be tuning for the rest of your life. You might as well learn to do it right the first time.

The easiest and most accurate way to tune is with a stroboscopic tuner. It's also very expensive, often cumbersome, and if you go somewhere with your guitar and forget your little black box, or if your batteries go dead, you have to eat pride and hand your guitar to a friend who knows how to tune *without* your magic meter. Unless you are a professional performer under pressure on stage, tuning with a strobe is like riding a bike with training wheels.

Much cheaper, almost as easy, and *much* less accurate is a pitch pipe. You blow through harmonica-like reeds that are supposed to match the pitches of the strings. Of course, like a harmonica, the pitch is determined quite a bit by how hard you blow. A soft breath gives you a lower note than a harder breath. Also, the sound of a reed is quite different from the sound of a string, and some people have trouble hearing if the string and reed are playing the same note.

By far, the best way to tune your guitar is with a tuning fork. It's cheap, portable, accurate, and doesn't need batteries. There's got to be a catch, right? There is. It gives you only one note. You have to find the rest on your own. Of course, if you ever decide to play with somebody else, say with someone playing a piano, dulcimer, tuba, or tromba marina, tuning your whole guitar to one note can be a useful skill.

Most tuning forks give you an "A440." That means those little metal legs wiggle 440 times each second when you hit them on something soft and firm (such as a knee), giving you the note some official decided to call "A." Tuning forks which play the note "E," specifically for guitars, are also available. "A" is more common because more instruments have A strings than E strings. The violin, viola, cello, bass, and guitar all have A strings, while only violin, bass and guitar have E strings.

The best way to tune with a fork is by *harmonics*. While it takes a lot of practice to get good at it, the effort is well worth it. It's the gateway to guitar wizardry.

A harmonic is a tone produced from a string that has been divided evenly into segments (two halves, three thirds, four fourths, etc.). You start these tones by touching the right place on the string as it is being plucked. This right place is called a **node**. Touching the string at a node stops it from vibrating at that point.

First try: take a fingertip of your left hand and just barely touch a string at the point marked off by the 12th fret. Classic and flamenco guitars join the neck and body at the 12th fret, while others join at the 14th fret and mark the 12th fret with some sort of inlay so it is easy to find. This inlay is called a **position marker**.

Touch it exactly over the metal fret—not down a little as if you were going to actually fret the note. Touch it with only the very tip

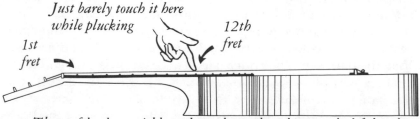

Just barely touch it here while plucking

1st fret

12th fret

Then softly, but quickly, release the touch and remove the left hand.

of your finger just hard enough so that one spot on the string doesn't vibrate. Now pluck the string with the right hand. You should hear a bell-like tone an octave above the note you hear if you play the open string.

Try playing the open unfretted string again, then the octave (12th fret) harmonic, over and over again until it gets easy to make that tone. You may release the touch of the left hand once the string is plucked. For some mystical reason, the string will not begin to vibrate at a node once the harmonic has begun.

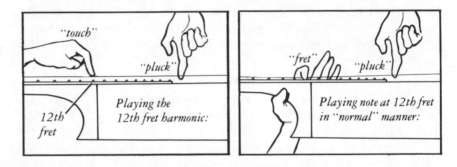

"touch"

"pluck"

12th fret

Playing the 12th fret harmonic:

"fret"

"pluck"

Playing note at 12th fret in "normal" manner:

A note to guitarists with movable bridges: If your bridge has slipped out of place, or even totally off your guitar, playing octave harmonics can help you place the bridge where it ought to be. On jazz guitars the little notches in the middle of the "f" holes roughly mark the location of the bridge. Place the bridge between these two notches. Get the strings roughly tuned to the right notes (get a friend to help if you don't know how yet). Next, play the octave harmonic on the skinniest string, then play the note, fretting the 12th fret as in normal guitar playing. (Push down between the 11th and 12 frets until the string touches the 12th fret, then pluck the string while holding the string against the 12th fret). They should be the same note. If they aren't you need to move the bridge until they are. If the fretted note is higher pitched than the harmonic, the bridge needs to go toward the tailpiece. If the fretted note is lower than the harmonic, the bridge needs to go toward the fingerboard.

Once you get the skinniest string right, check the fattest string the same way. If this string is off, try to slant the bridge so you move the end under the bass string without moving the bridge from where it's supposed to be under the treble (skinniest) string. Eventually, you should check all the strings, fudging the bridge around for the best overall location. It's normal to have the bass side of the bridge a tad closer to the tailpiece than the treble side.

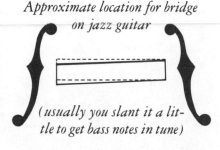

Approximate location for bridge on jazz guitar

(*usually you slant it a little to get bass notes in tune*)

Now, where were we? Oh yes. Now you can play octave harmonics, right? If you can't, go back and work on it until you can. The other harmonics are slightly more difficult to play.

Try playing a harmonic on the 7th fret. As you touch the string at the 7th fret, be careful not to be plucking the string at the 19th fret. If you do so, the Harmonics god will be displeased and will not sing for you.

Actually, the node at the 7th fret divides the string into three equal parts. To have three separately vibrating sections of string, you need two nodes to divide them. The other one is at the 19th fret. You get the same sound playing a harmonic at the 19th fret as at the 7th.

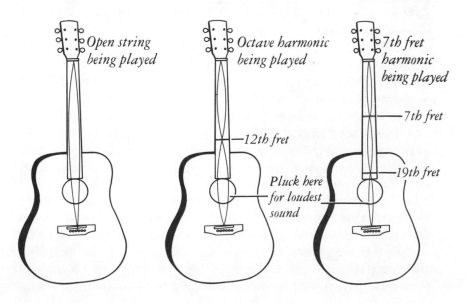

Open string being played

Octave harmonic being played

—*12th fret*

Pluck here for loudest sound

7th fret harmonic being played

—*7th fret*

—*19th fret*

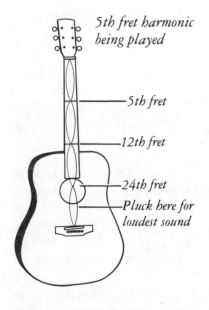

5th fret harmonic being played

5th fret

12th fret

24th fret

Pluck here for loudest sound

This can be fun. Enjoy it for a while. Try different strings. Play the octave harmonics. Try both the 7th and 19th frets. Try to get as clear a tone as you can. Pause now and then to sniff the sound-hole (most guitars smell good). Talk and sing softly into the soundhole. Enjoy yourself. Play the harmonics again. Play. The more you are at ease with this guitar, the better you will eventually play it.

Now try playing the harmonic at the 5th fret. This starts nodes at both the 12th fret and what would be the 24th fret if you had one—that's somewhere in the soundhole. See if you can find it by playing the harmonic there, matching it to the note of the 5th fret harmonic. The string is now divided into four parts.

That's as far as you need to go. Now you can tune your guitar by comparing the notes sounded by different strings playing these different harmonics.

Before that, we'll try a tad of music theory: Most folks know how to sing the musical scale, *do, re, mi, fa, sol, la, ti, do*. If you have trouble with that, I think you need to ask around. It's a little hard to convey in written form.

Now, we need an analogy. Imagine a staircase with eight steps, each one named after a note in our scale. If you and a friend stand on the bottom (*do*) step, there is zero distance between you. This is called a *unison*. You are both on the first scale step, and if you both sing that one note, we say you are singing in unison.

Now, leave your friend on the first step, and step up to the second (*re*) step. Now there is distance between you. If you each sing the note your step is named after (*do* and *re*) you aren't singing the same note anymore. The musical distance between you is called a *second*. The distance between *do* and *mi* is called a *third*. *Do* and *fa* makes a *fourth*. *Do* and *sol* makes a *fifth*.

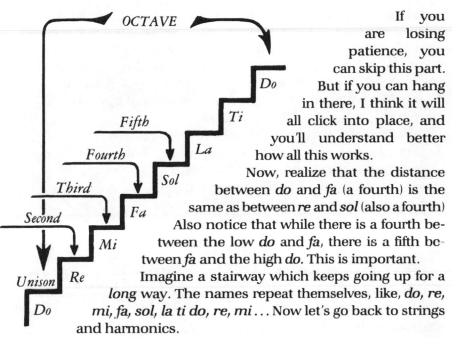

If you are losing patience, you can skip this part. But if you can hang in there, I think it will all click into place, and you'll understand better how all this works.

Now, realize that the distance between *do* and *fa* (a fourth) is the same as between *re* and *sol* (also a fourth) Also notice that while there is a fourth between the low *do* and *fa*, there is a fifth between *fa* and the high *do*. This is important.

Imagine a stairway which keeps going up for a *long* way. The names repeat themselves, like, *do, re, mi, fa, sol, la ti do, re, mi* ... Now let's go back to strings and harmonics.

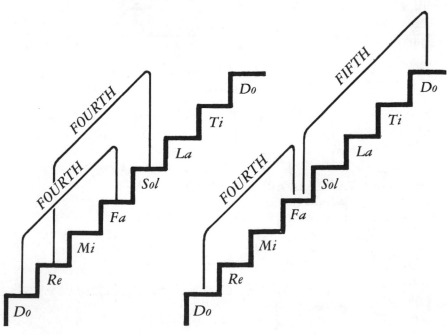

When you play an open string—let's say the lowest, fattest string—you are on the lowest step of our scale (the low *do*). When you play the 12th fret harmonic of that string, you skip up one octave to the next *do*. When you go to the 7th fret harmonic, you go up to the next *sol* (a fifth). When you play the 5th fret harmonic, you go up to the next *do*, a fourth up from *sol* and two octaves above the original *do*.

So what? Look at the drawings and reread the text until it makes a little sense. The missing link is that the musical distance of a fourth is between the lowest pitched string and the next one. This is the same musical distance we encountered between the 7th fret harmonic and the 5th fret harmonic.

So, if the sixth string (the fattest one) is tuned to *do*, the fifth string ought to be tuned to *fa*. This all boils down to the 5th fret harmonic of

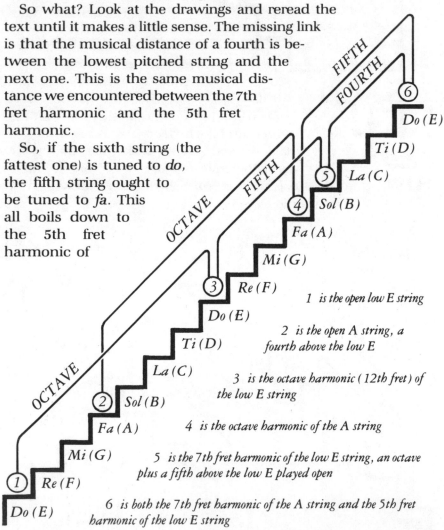

1 is the open low E string

2 is the open A string, a fourth above the low E

3 is the octave harmonic (12th fret) of the low E string

4 is the octave harmonic of the A string

5 is the 7th fret harmonic of the low E string, an octave plus a fifth above the low E played open

6 is both the 7th fret harmonic of the A string and the 5th fret harmonic of the low E string

the sixth string playing the exact same note as the 7th fret harmonic of the fifth string. Got that? Remember, the page will wait forever. Don't rush yourself. Take one step at a time. Go back again as often as it takes.

If you can't get it, don't worry. You can tune a guitar without all this, though you won't understand *why* things work as they do. At the end of all this theory, I'll give you a theory-free description of how to tune by harmonics, and an alternate, though less accurate method for those who can't get the hang of harmonics at all.

Without getting into *sharps* and *flats* quite yet, I'd like to explain what those letters A, B, C, D, E, F, and G are in music. Notice that there are seven different letters, and in our scale, we had seven different names (*do* repeated itself to make an eighth step). We could just as easily have named each step A, B, C, D, E, F, G, A, B, C, . . . The difference is that *do, re, mi,* . . . is what we call a *relative* scale, meaning we could be sitting in the middle of a meadow, miles away from anything like a tuned musical instrument, and arbitrarily start on any note, and call it *do*, and nobody would be able to say we were wrong. Once we establish what *do* is, however, all of those other names get assigned to particular pitches a certain *relative* distance from *do*.

The note A, on the other hand, is what you hear when the legs of a tuning fork wiggle 440 times a second. That particular note and octaves of that note are the only ones that rightfully can be called A. This is called an *absolute* scale.

It's like saying something is so many feet above the ground (a relative scale) or so many feet above sea level (an absolute scale). Mountains and valleys move ground level up and down, but sea level is sea level wherever you go.

So let's go back to the guitar. The open strings from the bass to treble are E, A, D, G, B, E. (Ellen Always Does Go to Bed Early.) (Or, from treble to bass, Every Body Gets Drunk At Elections.)

If you treat the letters like steps, you can determine the musical distance between them. E, f, g, A. That's a fourth. A, b, c, D. That's also a fourth. D, e, f, G. Again, a fourth. G, a, B. Another fourth? No, that's a third. B, c, d, E. Back to a fourth again.

Go over it until it makes sense, or give up. You can tune a guitar even if you don't understand why. I enjoy understanding why, and I'd like to give anybody who is interested the chance at that same enjoyment.

Your open A string sounds two octaves below an "A440" tuning fork. Play the 5th fret harmonic of the A string, and it should match the pitch of the fork.

How do you get it to match? Well, we've been out there in the outer spaces of theory and now we find ourselves on earth with a guitar and a tuning fork, not quite sure what to do with either. If you don't have a tuning fork yet, what are you waiting for? You need one now. Preferably A440.

A BRIEF DIGRESSION IN FORK APPRECIATION

A tuning fork is an interesting creature. This strangely shaped hunk of metal plays only one note, but it is the most stable acoustic source of a single pitch yet invented. The idea is to hold it by the single short leg and hit one of the long legs on something like your knee, or the heel of your shoe. The note may seem very soft if you just hold the fork out in open space, but if you press the end of the single short leg to the

bridge of the guitar, it's plenty loud to tune to. It can also be heard played on a tabletop by touching the end to it. If you touch the end of the short leg of the fork to your skull, especially right behind your ear or in the center just above your forehead, you'd be surprised how loud it is. Perhaps the loudest place to touch it, though it gives some folks the creeps, is your teeth.

It's game time, folks, and the tuning fork is another toy. It would be a real shame to own one of these critters for a couple of years and never have experienced just how much fun it can be. It's especially fun to dunk the forked end into a glass of water. Large tuning forks splash when they touch. Whimpier forks merely ripple the surface, but even that's pretty neat because the ripples *don't move.* When was the last time you saw unfrozen water wrinkle without quivering? And if you dip it deeper into the water, sometimes it makes a weird noise. Experiment. This is how Edison started.

Okay, so I'm still a kid at heart. So what? If more grown-ups learned healthy ways to play, we wouldn't have wars. We'd be too busy dipping our tuning forks.

After all this, the way I use it is to hold the forked end pointed at my ear. It's easy to do, and I can hear it better, in a way that lets me compare the note to that of the guitar.

Here's where you get to build up your grace and efficiency of motion. After you've played with your tuning fork for a while, you'll learn that it doesn't sustain a loud note very long. If you take too long getting set up to hear your guitar string and the fork together, the note on the fork dies before you get to use it. To combat this, learn the motions I next describe and practice them until they flow smoothly. This will give you all the time you need.

First, get a good, comfortable, hugging grip on the guitar. Do it in a way that frees both hands to do other things than hold the guitar. My favorite is to sit the waist of the guitar on my left thigh with the lower bout cradled between my legs. I lean a little forward so my chest meets the back of the guitar at the upper bout, and my right elbow lightly presses the lower bout on the top. That's a pretty secure grip, leaving me with all the freedom I need.

Next, think about what your left hand has to do. First it must touch the fifth string at the 5th fret. As soon as the note is sounded, the left hand then moves to adjust the tuning button for the A string.

The right hand has to hold the tuning fork between the thumb and index finger while using the ring finger to pluck the string for the harmonic. As soon as the note is sounded, the right hand must strike the tuning fork on the knee, or whatever, and place the tuning fork where it will be heard (pointed at your ear, or touching the guitar bridge, your skull, or teeth).

Think it through and practice, slowly at first. It is more important to learn to do it smoothly than to try being fast right off the bat. Concentrating on speed before learning coordination promotes a jerky, whipping motion which leads to dropping the fork, turning the wrong tuner, dropping the guitar, falling out of your chair, or other *swift* moves you wouldn't want to have to explain to anyone who might wander by or overhear from the next room.

Once you are good enough at this (not falling out of your chair), you need to know what to listen for. Most folks can tell when the string is far out of pitch. If you know it's way off, but aren't quite sure whether it's sharp (too high pitched) or flat (too low pitched), it might help to imagine singing the pitch of the string, then of the fork. Which one made your throat feel tighter? Match the notes as closely as you can. When it gets close, something interesting happens. When two notes are *very* close, but not quite in tune, there is a pulsing change in the volume. We call this *beats*. It's that "wowowowow" sound. The idea is to get rid of the beats. As you move toward the right pitch, the beats slow down. If you go in the wrong direction, the beats speed up. If you go in the right direction, but go too far, the beats slow down, then speed up again.

This is the big advantage of tuning by harmonics. Since the harmonic note keeps ringing after you remove your left hand from the string, you can tune the note while you listen to it; instead of listening, then killing the note, tuning it, then plucking to see if you went far enough or too far. You can listen for beats while you twist the tuning button and tune the string.

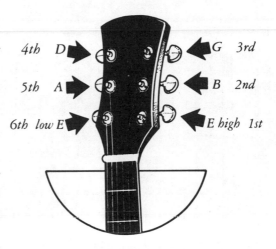

4th D

5th A

6th low E

G 3rd

B 2nd

E high 1st

If you have kept up with me to now, your A string should be in tune with the fork. Now we have to get the Low E string in tune with the A. Sound the 7th fret harmonic of the fifth (A) string, then the 5th fret harmonic of the sixth string. This should be the same note.

Why? You are playing two octaves above the E string, and one octave plus a fifth above the A string. The A is a fourth above the E, and a fourth plus a fifth is an octave (E plus a fourth is A, A plus a fifth is E). Both strings play the E two octaves above the low E string played open. If you're having trouble, look over the illustrations. Take your time. The book waits *forever*.

It just so happens that like the 5th fret harmonic on the low E string, the high E string is two octaves above the open low E string. So after you tune the low E to the A, tune the open high E to the 5th fret harmonic of the low E string. Got it?

The 7th fret harmonic of the low E string is an octave and a fifth above the open note. If you count that out (E, f, g, a, B—a fifth) you get the same note as the open B string. Yes?

You have now tuned 4 of the 6 strings. Proud yet? The rest is fairly easy. The 7th fret harmonic of the D needs to match the 5th fret harmonic of the A, which is already in tune. The 7th fret harmonic of the G string must match the 5th fret harmonic of the D. And that's it. Check the pictures for review.

WHAT TO MATCH WHEN TUNING
The arrows go from the note which is right to the note which must be changed to match it.

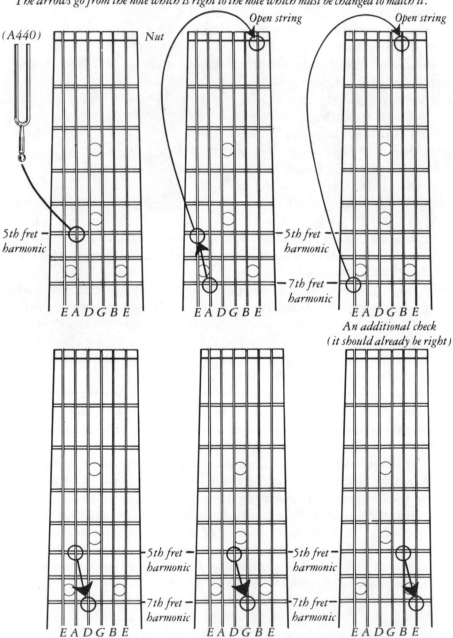

Theory-Free Tuning

For those of you who skipped the theory, you need to have read far enough to know how to play harmonics at both the 5th and 7th fret. Okay? The 5th fret harmonic of the A string and the tuning fork should both play A440.

Hold the tuning fork in your right hand between your thumb and forefinger, and play the harmonic by plucking the A string with your middle or ring finger. The note will be louder if you pluck it between the bridge and soundhole rather than in the soundhole.

As soon as you hear the note of the harmonic, move your left hand to take hold of the tuner for the A string, and use your right hand to strike the tuning fork on your knee, or whatever, then put the tuning fork where you can hear it (pointed at your ear, pressed against the bridge of the guitar, pressed against your teeth, etc.).

Get a feel for these two separate sources of sound. Most likely, they won't be making the same note, especially if the guitar is not freshly tuned. Tune the A string until it roughly matches the fork. Again, it may help to imagine singing the two notes to feel which makes your throat tighter.

Once the two notes are close, they'll make a sound sort of like: "wowowowowowow." We call that *beats*. You have to get rid of the beats, or else your audience beats you 'cause you're out of tune.

The beats can guide you to the right pitch. As you approach the right pitch, the beats slow down. If you go too far, they speed up again. Basically, if they speed up, you are going the wrong way. Play with it until "wowowowowowow" becomes "wooooooooo."

So, you use beats to match the 5th fret harmonic of the A string to the tuning fork. Then you play the 7th fret harmonic of that A string and tune the low E string until its 5th string harmonic matches it.

Once the low E is tuned, play the 5th fret harmonic of the low E again, this time tuning the high E string until its open note matches the harmonic of the low E. The open B string should match the 7th fret harmonic of the low E string in the same way.

Now tune the D string to the A so that the D string's 7th fret harmonic matches the A's 5th fret harmonic. Tune the G string to the D in the same way (the 7th fret harmonic of the G matches the 5th fret harmonic of the D).

Now go find a friend or family member to bother and show off how you can tune your guitar. You might want to practice a little before you embarass yourself, but then a little embarassment will probably drive you to practice harder than if you got it right the first time.

Tuning without Harmonics

For those of you who don't believe that harmonics really exist, or for some other reason choose not to use them, you can play normally fretted strings to tune. Press the string to the fret with your finger on the nut side of the fret so you don't go "thud" instead of "ding." The fifth fret of one string plays the same note of the next higher positioned string played open, except that the 4th fret of the G string plays the open B string.

For this method of tuning, it's easier if you start out tuning the low E. Try to get an E tuning fork, a piano, or a friend on another instrument to give you an E note. If all you have is an A tuning fork, tune the open A string, then match the 5th fret of the low E string to the open A.

Fretting a string at the 5th fret:

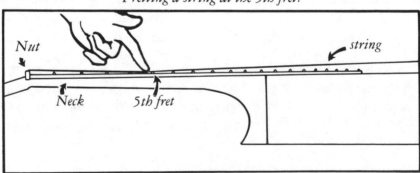

Either way, once the E and A strings are tuned, playing the note of the 5th fret on the A string gives you the note of the open D string. The 5th fret of the D gives you the open G. The 4th fret of the G gives you the B. The 5th fret of the B gives you the high E. Play the high E and the low E. Here's where you learn about the difference between theory and reality. There's a good chance that the high and low Es will not be in tune with each other, and they need to be in tune. You may have tuned each string very slightly off and all of those little mistakes add up to a bigger error which shows up to your ear between the high E and low E. You will need to try to tune it over again and again until the two Es match and every other string is pretty much in tune with its neighboring strings. Sometimes this requires a little fudging.

While tuning this way, keep in mind that if you squeeze too tightly on a string while playing it, you raise the pitch slightly. It throws things off even worse if you slide your finger slightly to one side while fretting a note. That's how rock 'n rollers *bend* notes in wailing guitar solos. It might sound great in a hot guitar riff, but it doesn't help get things in tune one little bit.

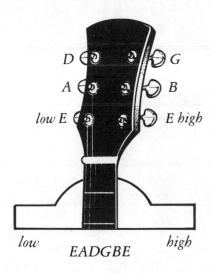

As you play guitar, you will most likely develop *an ear for tuning*, which means you'll probably find several different ways to check your tuning and will get to where you adjust certain notes without even thinking about what you are listening for.

CHAPTER 5

Changing Strings

How often should you change strings? Over the years people have asked me that and I still don't think there's a *right* answer. Very simply, change them as often as you can afford the money and the time. New strings take a brief breaking-in period, then they are wonderful. Then they slowly lose that ring and become dull, and they get worse the longer you play them. If you play them until they break, you're putting up with dull strings that often don't play well even in tune. Spots stretch and dent, making the string vary in thickness and heaviness along the length, so a string that is in tune when played open can be out of tune when it is fretted. If your strings break often, notice *where* they break. Sometimes the nut or saddle might be a tad too sharp.

Steel strings also corrode, creating an effect similar to raking your fingers across miniature barbed wire. Some people have naturally corrosive sweat oozing from their fingertips and will have to change steel strings more often.

You can make changing strings a ritual of peaceful celebration. It represents doing something special for something you care about. The reward comes when you sit to play and the experience sounds and feels much better.

How do you select strings? First, you must match the type (nylon or steel) suited for your guitar. If you've read this far in the book and still don't know which type guitar strings match your guitar, then I've failed. I haven't, have I?

What particular set of strings is best? Music stores carry steel strings in light, medium, and heavy gauge, silk 'n' steel and phosphor bronze. They have classic strings with or without a wound G string and bass strings wound with bronze or silver. Which particular brand should you buy? That's all a matter of taste. Different guitars react differently to the same set of strings, so the only thing to do is experiment.

There are Martin guitars with "scallopped" braces, which bear the following burned inscription legible through the soundhole. "Use only light gauge strings." Believe it. This guitar has its braces shaved thinner, as they used to do before medium and heavy gauge strings were invented. For the same reason any really old guitar should also use light gauge strings. The tops aren't braced heavily enough for the higher tension of heavier strings.

Heavier gauge strings provide a louder sound. That's their only excuse for existence. They also are rough on guitars and guitarists. Some guitars are built so heavily that they *need* heavy gauge strings to get any sound out of them.

The best advice is simple. Buy something; try it. Try something else. Which did you like better? Was it worth the money? It is the only way to learn the best choice of strings for both you and your guitar.

Now, how do you get the string from the package onto the guitar? First, let's think through exactly what we are doing to the guitar. We're starting with an old set of strings, tuned to proper pitch, tugging at the bridge and neck. Our goal is to replace them with new strings, also tuned to proper pitch, with the same tug in the same places.

If we pull off all of the old strings at once, then put on all of the new strings, we shift the stress in the neck joint back and forth, as if we were trying to tear the neck off the guitar. It's far better to remove one old string, put on its replacement and tune it. Then pull off another old string, etc. The higher pitched strings take longer to stretch out enough to hold pitch, so it makes sense to replace them first. Retune them each time you replace a new string in the bass.

Don't get the idea that you should replace each string on a different day. It's all done at one sitting, but the guitar shouldn't have more than one string removed at a time; it should always have at least five strings tuned up to pitch. If this rule is violated, the guitar will not instantly destroy itself; and certain repairs *require* removing all the strings at once. But the less often it happens, the better. Changing strings is not an excuse to treat the guitar in anything but a gentle manner. A guitar has to live through hundreds of string changes.

The most sensible way to change strings is to remove the high E string after tuning the entire old set of strings to a tuning fork. Put on the new high E—we'll get to details later. Tune it to its proper pitch.

Remove the B string. Put on the new B and tune it up to pitch. By the time the B is up to pitch the high E will have stretched, so you should tune it again. You should then tune the B again and the E again until both are *sort-of-almost* holding pitch.

Remove the G string and put on the new G. Tune it, the B, the high E, the G again, the B again, etc. Proceed in the same way for the D, A, and low E strings. Note that you won't need the tuning fork again until you tune the low E, because until then you'll have the old strings to which you may tune. The whole process often takes me half an hour, but it's well worth the time. Once this is done, even nylon strings (which stretch out a lot more than steel strings) hold pitch. You may replace strings faster, but you'll spend much time and frustration tuning afterward.

Always anchor new strings at the bridge or tailpiece *before* you worry about the end which goes to the tuning machines. Steel strings all have *balls* (they look like grooved metal doughnuts to me) at the bridge/tailpiece end of the string.

If your guitar has a tailpiece, before removing a string look at how the strings are already anchored there. Tune the high E string down until it is limp. Keep turning the tuning button until the string is loose enough to unwind from the roller at the tuning machine. Notice how the string is tied to the roller (if at all).

Once the string is free of the roller, you need only feed it back through the hole in the tailpiece to remove it from there. To put in the new string, just reverse the sequence for removing the string. Thread the new string through the hole in the tailpiece from the tail side and pull it until the ball jams at the hole. Stick the other end of the string through the hole in the roller and pull it until it's almost straight, but not tight. The string is intentionally too long. Wrap this excess string around the roller toward the inside and tuck it under that string where it goes *into* the hole in the roller (from the nut). Pull it back over the string to form a loop and crimp it. As you turn the tuning button, it will press the tightened string over this excess string enough to hold. A pair of wire cutters works well to trim off the excess string up close to the roller.

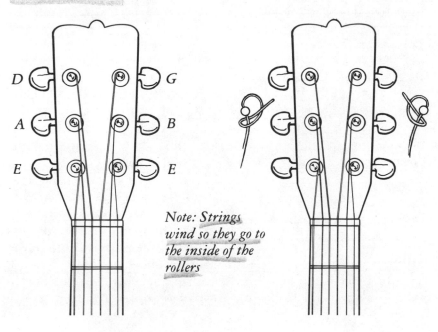

D   G

A   B

E   E

Note: Strings wind so they go to the inside of the rollers

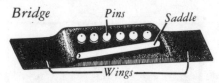

Bridge   Pins   Saddle

Wings

Steel-string guitars without tailpieces have the same type tuning head, but the ball end of the string is actually inside the body of the guitar. First tune down the high E string and unwrap it from the roller. Once that end is free, notice where the other end submerges into a tiny hole or slot in the bridge right next to a white plastic knob (bridge pin). Pull out that knob. It's probably a bit stiff, so you might need a small screwdriver to use gently as a lever to free it. Better yet, most music stores carry a plastic tool made specifically to pull bridge pins. Some versions double as a handle to aid cranking the tuning button while changing strings. These plastic tools are less likely to scar the saddle than a screwdriver.

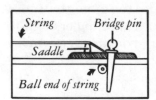

SIDE VIEW

String   Bridge pin

Saddle

Ball end of string

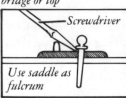

Careful not to scratch bridge or top

Screwdriver

Use saddle as fulcrum

Special tool used to pull pins

Once you have removed the bridge pin you will see that the hole is shaped like a keyhole. The ball should fit through the round part of the hole, tightly perhaps. Stuff the ball end of the new string into the hole, laying the string into the slot of the keyhole while stuffing the bridge pin back into the hole. You should line up the slot in the bridge pin with the slot in the hole. No need to press tightly. You may split the bridge if you do.

Tie Block   Saddle

Wings

Classic and Flamenco guitars use a bridge which differs from that of a steel-string guitar. The wings and saddle are much the same, though the strings usually have plain ends that are anchored on a tie block. This tie block is merely a raised, rectangular section of the bridge with holes drilled parallel to the top of the guitar. The knot used is traditional and usually holds well enough. Stick the string through the hole, bring it back over the tie block and wrap the end under the string where it first went *into* the hole. Now bring the string back over the tie block and tuck it under the string where it first came *out* of the hole.

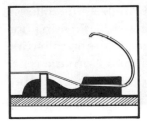 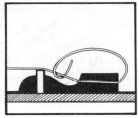 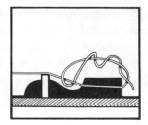

Let's review. The new string comes from the neck of the guitar, goes over the saddle into the hole (note: this is what I'm talking about when I say "where the string first goes into the hole"), and comes out of the hole on the side of the tie block farthest from the saddle (note: this is what I mean when I say "where the string first came out of the hole"). Now, it goes back over the tie block and wraps under the string where it first went into the hole. The end of the string is then brought over the tie block again, and tucked between the string and the tie block where the string first came out of the hole.

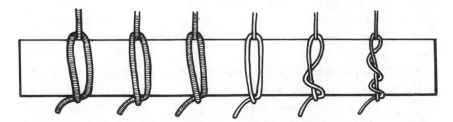

That's the basic knot which will hold for the bass strings. The treble strings are skinnier and slicker, especially the high E string (the skinniest). To hold them, you need to tie the same knot with a couple extra twists. As before, you stick the string in the hole, bring it out, and wrap it under the string where it first went into the hole. But now you must wrap it around that segment of string already over the tie block. Do this twice for the thinnest string, and once for the next thinnest string. Finish the knot with the tuck under the string where it first comes out of the hole. Pull the knot tight by pulling the string at the tuner end.

The rollers of a classic guitar are large enough to hold all of the excess string without you needing to clip off any of the length. Simply stick the end of the string through the hole in the roller so it protrudes perhaps 1/2" through the other side. Pressing one finger over either the in or out hole of the roller will stop the string from slipping while you turn the tuning buttons. Turn the roller in the right direction so that the string goes *over* the roller and not under it.

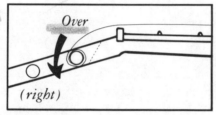
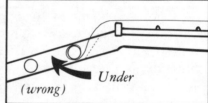

As the protruding end comes around to meet the string coming from the bridge, lay the protruding end to either side and pull the other end (from the bridge) tight enough to hold it in place. From here on you just keep winding, holding some tension on the string so long as it needs it. At least three windings should cover that 1/2" protrusion to hold it tight. Beyond that, neatness is its own reward.

One fine point: Notice that the innermost strings (the D and G) will scrape against the center of the tuning head between the slots unless you wrap the spools so that the strings come from the side of the spool nearest the tuning gears. Taking care to do this isn't extremely important, but it will minimize a worn spot on the tuning head where the string will otherwise scrape it when you tune, and theoretically it would make tuning a bit easier because the string will be pressed against one less surface.

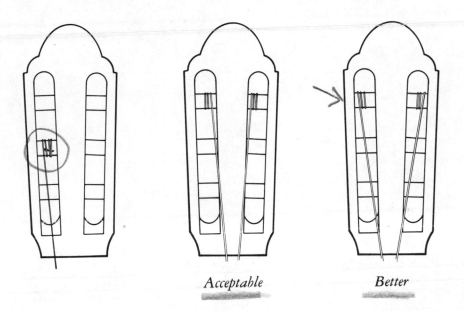

Acceptable   *Better*

CHAPTER 6

Adjustments

The Action

The spacial relationship between the strings and the finger-board is referred to as the **playing action**. Being in adjustment makes a huge difference between a guitar that is comfortable to play and one which interferes with your ability to sound like you want to sound.

If the neck is bowed to a convex curve, the instrument is use-less. But the more concave it is, the more difficult it is to play in higher positions. If it is too flat, the slightest unevenness in the frets causes a *buzz* while playing certain notes. If the strings are too close to the finger board, the action is too low and you get that same buzz if you play with any loudness at all. If it is too high, it overworks your left hand just to fret the notes. Somewhere be-tween these extremes is heaven.

If you buy a new guitar and the action is too high, you may be dissapointed; but if the guitar buzzes, you'll be irate and probably take it back to the store. Manufacturers know this. They also know that to accurately adjust the action of each guitar takes more time than they want to take, so they intentionally make the action too high. Because no single action height is right for every player, they figure that anyone bothered by a high action should be able to find a way to lower it to individual taste.

Some stores will tell you that they have someone who really knows his stuff, who individually adjusts every guitar they sell. Usually they still leave the action too high, for the same reasons. Better to have pain than buzzes.

My guitars neither have buzzes, nor cause pain. It's not really that difficult to achieve either. Just do it THE RIGHT way in THE RIGHT order. I'll show you how.

CAUTION: I have been warned that the idea of touching your guitar with files and wrenches will turn some people against me enough to not read further in the book. Realize that you *can* get a pro to do it for $$. You don't *have* to do it yourself. But for those who dare to venture onward to try this, these adjustments *are* reversible. The parts you'll be filing are cheap and easily replaceable at *no* detriment to your instrument.

NOTE: Read completely through a procedure before beginning to actually do anything.

ADJUSTING THE NECK

Skip this part if your guitar doesn't have an adjustable truss rod. Those necks are already all they'll ever be. Go to the section on "Adjusting the Nut."

If you do have an adjustable neck, check to see how flat the fingerboard is. The truss rod should be used to adjust the flatness of the fingerboard. It shall not be used to adjust the height of the action. If you believe otherwise, just try it. You'll discover that when you adjust it one way, you get a curve. When you adjust it the other way, you get a *reverse* curve. Between these two is flat, or at least as close to flat as *this* guitar will ever see. Most guitar necks adjust between simple convex and concave curves, but the wood sometimes reacts to this balance between the string tension and the truss rod by forming complex curves, such as an "S." Remember that your goal is nearly flat, with a *slight* tendency toward the concave.

Most truss rod adjustment screws are accessible only after removing a small plastic cover near the nut on the tuning head.

77

Allen wrenches may be purchased in sets at hardware stores and such. Different guitars require different allen wrench sizes, while others require regular screwdrivers or wrenches. My best advice is to pull off the cover and figure out what you need for the adjustment, then get it.

Adjusting the truss rod often involves a couple of unexpected tasks. You may have to remove the strings to remove the cover for the truss adjustment. With metal strings, removal often means replacement because the old string often has a dent where it bent coming out of the nut. Taking down the string tension and then tuning back up to pitch sometimes breaks the string. Because you can't really adjust the truss rod without a full set of strings tuned up to pitch, you'd best start out with an extra set of strings . . . or two. It's worth it.

As the illustration on page 41 showed, some guitars have truss rods which emerge from the soundhole end of the neck instead of from the tuning head end. Manufacturers usually choose to do this if they want their guitars to look like Martins because a Martin tuning head has no plastic plate on it. The truss rod works the same way wherever the adjustment screw is located.

The truss rod pulls the neck in the direction opposite to the string tension. The threads on the rod are like any other screw, so if the fingerboard is overly concave (pulled up by the strings), tighten the adjustment clockwise (a difficult concept, perhaps, in an age of digital watches). Loosen it (counterclockwise) if the neck is bowed backwards (convex).

Before and after each adjustment, tune all of the strings up to pitch and check the neck as you did in the *test drive*—that is fret each string at the first fret and the highest fret together, and use the string as a straight edge to see how flat the neck is. Before doing the adjustment, lower the tension on all the strings so there will be less tension on the truss rod and the adjustment screw will be easier to turn. Depending on how picky you are, you may have to take the string tension up and down and make slight adjustments to the truss rod many times. It's a bit tedious, but the better you do this now, the less likely you'll have to do it again—and the better the playing action, the better the guitar. Basically, you want to have the string not *quite* touch the 7th-9th frets as you hold both ends of the string against the highest and lowest frets.

ADJUSTING THE NUT

The nut is that grooved white plastic (bone or ivory on classier instruments) piece residing betwixt the fingerboard and the tuning head. It determines how high off the first fret the strings stand as you play the string *open* (unfretted).

Most guitars have a nut that is entirely too high. Why? If the nut is too low, strings buzz when played open. Again, manufacturers don't have the time to adjust it perfectly, so they choose to make it too high.

Too high means you'll need to give the strings a little more *squeeze* to play lower position notes. If this is your first guitar, you'll be playing *only* lower position notes for a while. More squeeze means more pain for your fingertips, and though you may not notice it, the notes will play a little sharp.

So, how high is right? Hold the guitar in your lap like you're going to play it. Use a finger of your right hand to press the string of your choice against the highest fret. Now with a finger of your

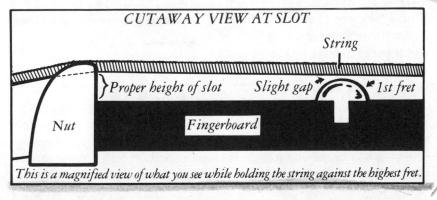

CUTAWAY VIEW AT SLOT

String

Proper height of slot — Slight gap — 1st fret

Nut — Fingerboard

This is a magnified view of what you see while holding the string against the highest fret.

left hand fret that same string at the 3rd fret. If you slide your finger on the left hand to the 2nd fret, the string doesn't rise up much off the 3rd fret. Right? Slip that finger to the 1st fret and it also doesn't rise much. Remove your left hand, however, and it rises much more. Tada! It shouldn't.

Your quest is to bring the string infinitely close to touching the first fret *without* touching it when you hold the other end of the string down per instructions in the previous paragraph. If you succeed you will not have any more buzzes playing the open string than you will while playing the string fretted at the first fret. Got it?

Adjustment is done with a small narrow file. Look in hobby shops and hardware stores for one that will fit into the groove of the nut. You don't want to lower the entire nut, you want to lower each string separately. Get a file or a pair of files to cut both downward into the groove and to the sides to widen the groove.

The most important thing is to get really familiar with the string you're working on and the tiny space between it and the fingerboard. Make sure the string is tuned up to pitch. If it's tuned low, the string will be too high and you'll cut the slot too deep, which takes a lot of work to fix. That's fact, not theory.

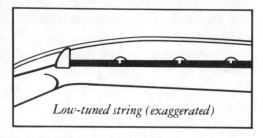

Low-tuned string (exaggerated)

Again, with your right hand press a string down until it touches the fret nearest the soundhole.

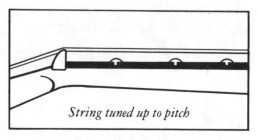

String tuned up to pitch

Now inspect the gap between that string and the fret nearest the nut. In your head take the present space and subtract the gap between the string and the first fret. This will give you an image of how big the space *should* be between the bottom of the nut slot and the fingerboard. Once you have a *clear* image of this, you may continue.

Remove the string. Begin to file away at the bottom of the slot, holding the file at a slight angle so

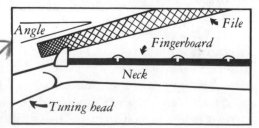

Angle

File

Fingerboard

Neck

Tuning head

the edge of the nut nearest the fingerboard is the highest point in the slot.

Don't *quite* cut the slot as deep as your *clear* image tells you to. It takes less time to arrive at a proper adjustment by four filings that are each too shallow than by one that is too deep.

Replace the string and tune it to pitch. Check your work. If it's still too high, start over. If it's just right, go on to another string. If you finish all the strings and don't cut *any* of them too low, congratulations. Proceed to adjust the saddle.

If you filed one or more of the slots too deep, it or they will buzz when you play the open note. That's not good, my friend, but it is repairable. Here's how. Get some glue and a splinter of hardwood, and some manner of clamp or weight. You need to fill the slot and make a new, shallow one. Though I've always used wood, I've heard that a drop of epoxy can also be used. Epoxy would simply be dripped into the slot to fill it, whereas wood with wood glue (Elmers or Tightbond works fine) requires clamping, so you'll also need to pad the clamp to avoid marring the neck. The splinter should more than fill the slot. Later, you will file it flush with the nut and file a new slot into the splinter.

If you've cut slots too deep and can't manage to fill them, you may either place shims under the nut, or you may buy a

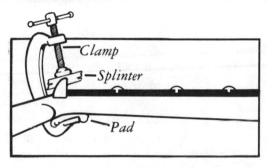

Clamp
—Splinter
—Pad

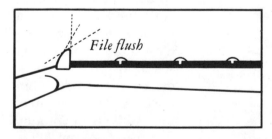

File flush

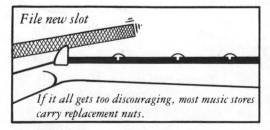

File new slot

If it all gets too discouraging, most music stores carry replacement nuts.

new nut. Take your guitar to a music store and make sure the nut you buy matches your guitar. Now you may hire a luthier to adjust your new nut, or you may start the task again yourself.

The Saddle

This adjustment is the most subjective of the Big Three (neck, nut and saddle). The saddle is the slotless white piece which the strings go over at the bridge. Its height determines the height of the overall action. Too high means less ease of playing, especially in the upper positions. Too low means buzzing when you play at full volume. If you play loudly, you'll need a higher action. Nylon strings require a much higher action than steel strings. What's right for you depends very largely on how you play. It's best to look at a few guitars to get a feel for the range, then experiment a little, and perhaps gamble a little. Remember, if you adjust too far, you can reverse the adjustment, though it is a more involved task.

To lower the saddle, remove all of the strings. The saddle should now have nothing holding it in place except a snug fit—no glue. You should file away at the *bottom* of the saddle—the part you can't see until you have removed the saddle from the bridge. The bottom of the saddle is often quite rough and uneven. Filing it flat will improve the tone of the guitar by giving more contact between the saddle (which carries all the string vibrations) and the top (which does all of the acoustic amplifying).

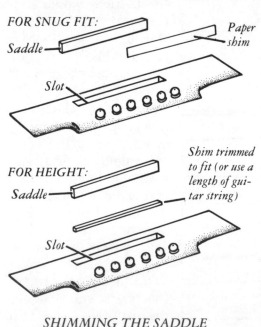

FOR SNUG FIT:
Saddle
Paper shim
Slot

Shim trimmed to fit (or use a length of guitar string)

FOR HEIGHT:
Saddle
Slot

SHIMMING THE SADDLE

82

Also, keep in mind that the treble strings can be lower than the bass strings without buzzing.

Like the nut, it's a matter of filing, replacing the strings, tuning and testing. Repeat adjustments when necessary.

If you lower the action more than you wish, you'll need to place a shim—preferably of some hardwood veneer—into the slot in the bridge under the saddle. Paper may be used, but it doesn't conduct sound as well. Also use shims if the saddle fits loosely in its slot. Shim the sides of the saddle until it is snug. As Cowboy Bob once said, "the snugger the saddle, the better." Sound energy gets wasted by a wiggling saddle. Loose saddles also often sag and lean toward the neck. This causes the string length to be a little short, so it doesn't quite play in tune. If you *really* need to raise the saddle a *lot*, or if you don't like the idea of using shims, you may replace the saddle altogether. Most music stores carry them. Remember to take either the guitar or the old saddle with you.

Altering the Tone

While you're getting your hands to work and removing strings, let's discuss what can be done to change the sound of your instrument. Realize that in this area, *everything* is experimental. If you like the sound of your instrument, and especially if it is valuable, *leave the inside alone*. This section is solely for those who want a very personal relationship with an instrument with which they might be willing to gamble a bit.

My experience in this area began when I bought a steel-string folk guitar. I already had a wonderful classic guitar, and I didn't have funds to invest in nearly as good a folk guitar. What I bought sounded nice in the treble, but the bass sounded as if it were stuffed with dirty socks.

My classic guitar had an unusually even balance between the treble and the bass. The man who made it explained that he accomplished that by using an asymetrical design with heavy braces on the treble side and light braces on the bass side. I felt around inside to get a good idea of what he was describing.

The result of this design is that the tap tone—the note you hear when you thump the wood lightly with a knuckle—is lower on the bass side of the bridge than on the treble side. Checking the new steel-string guitar, I discovered that the tap tone was the same all over the bridge. I tried carving away on the major brace on the bass side of the soundboard. The tap tone on the bass side of the bridge lowered slightly. I went back several times, carving on this brace and other smaller ones in the area. I even took some shavings off the inside of the soundboard itself. The tap tone lowered each time. When I restrung the guitar, I noticed that the bass tone of the instrument had improved considerably with no reduction in treble quality.

Anyone comtemplating this course of action should realize that it also weakens the top and shortens the life of the guitar. I figured, however, that a long life was useless for a guitar that sounded like mine when I bought it.

By similar logic, if your guitar has a thin treble sound, you might try adding some spruce bracing on the treble side. You can get such wood at a luthier supply house or anywhere that would carry wood for musical instrument. Begin your search by asking music stores. Again, realize that results are unpredictable. Don't risk a good guitar.

Recently I played a guitar made by a friend which had an extremely resonant bass (a little boomy for my taste), which he demonstrated to come primarily from an extremely thin back. Next time I have the strings off my folk guitar, I intend to thin the back a bit, since the instrument is still quite underwhelming below the low A. Make your own judgments. It is *your* instrument. The positive or negative consequences will be yours to bear alone.

I have read articles which promote adding weight to the neck and tuning head of guitars. Normally, it seems that a guitar neck flexes very slightly with the vibrations of the string. The lighter the neck and head, the less resistance it has to this wiggling, so sound energy gets used up by the neck, which is not as good at projecting sound as the soundboard. This gives you a shorter sustain and softer volume.

I would cite the specific articles to give credit where it is due, and to avoid any misgiven paraphasing, but I read these articles in friends' magazines, in doctors' offices and on news stands. I frankly don't remember the source, though I do remember reading *different* articles describing *different* experiments, all of which came to the same conclusion: The heavier the neck and tuning head, the louder the guitar and the longer the notes are sustained. There also comes a point at which the guitar becomes very uncomfortable to play. Topple, thud.

If you find this intriguing, have at it. You may be as refined as having a luthier bury hidden weights beneath veneer or do decorative inlays of metal, or you might get crude and clamp a brick to your tuning head. I'm quite happy without *any* of this, but some of you might feel differently.

CHAPTER 7

Repairs

Realize that it is nearly always better to seek a professional repairperson than to try to do a major repair yourself. Unfortunately, many of us can't afford that, and if you can handle the risk of what you might do to the instrument, there really is a special feeling that comes from fixing your own guitar. Do realize that if you begin a substantial repair and *then* seek a pro to finish it for you, or to correct your mistake, he or she may make a voodoo doll that looks a lot like you. He or she also will probably charge you more than if you had not started the repair yourself, and will spend more time meditating (perhaps months) before beginning the repair because he or she must first figure out how to fix *your* repair before facing the problem you tried to fix in the first place. Face it, *if you begin a repair, you have to face it yourself. Don't write me angry letters. Don't be indignant to the repairperson who must unscramble your deed. I do not recommend that you do all of your own repairs. I am trying to provide information to those who need it.*

How to pick out a luthier? The yellow pages are a good start if you don't already know of one. It is also good to ask any musician friends. It's always good to either see some of the work that the luthier has done, or at least talk to someone who had an instru-

ment fixed by him or her. Musical instrument repair is an incon
sistant field where even individual repairpersons often do inconsistent work.

Neck Joint Repairs

Most of you will not want to do this. For a non-professional it
takes a certain amount of raw nerve. It's safer to have an experienced luthier do it, but . . .

There are several designs for neck-to-body joints on guitars
these days, and the number increases as technology sacrifices
acoustics and aesthetics. There are two joints traditionally used
for guitars.

The *Spanish* neck joint is used most commonly in hand built
classic and flamenco guitars. So far as I know, nobody mass
produces this joint, and few luthers dare to repair it, either. It is by

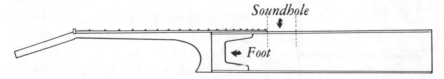

far the strongest joint and probably is best at conducting sound to
the body from the neck. You can recognize it by the *foot*, which is
an extension of the neck block inside the guitar. It may be easily
seen through the soundhole.

The neck block is an extension of the neck, with the sides of the
guitar glued into slots cut into the sides of this block. The back is
glued to the bottom of this block and the top of the guitar is glued
to the top of this block. I've never heard of one of these joints
breaking. It is solid.

Most mass-produced guitars and some handmade guitars use
what's called a *tapered dovetail joint.* The body of the guitar is
built to completion with the neck block inside, and the neck is
built to completion with a protruding dovetail at the end where
you usually see a guitar body. A special router jig is used to cut a
slot into the body at the neck block to fit the dovetail of the neck.

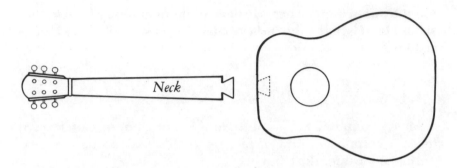

This joint is a lot easier to make with power tools and it requires less fitting and careful alignment than the Spanish joint, but it is not nearly as solid. The back of the joint doesn't even touch, leaving a gap, so the sides of the slot have all the glue surface that holds the joint.

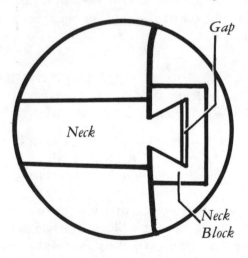

Some guitar factory workers apparently are ignorant of this. I've repaired several guitars with lots of glue on the back surface of the neck block, and very little on the sides of the slot which hold the neck on.

Jay, a friend and a very respected repairman and luthier, reminds me that someone might read this next suggestion and begin tearing the neck off a $1,000 Martin. Please consider the value of the instrument *before* you decide whether to do a repair yourself or hire a pro. Realize that professional repairpersons often have special tools to inject steam into such a neck joint to loosen the glue. They also have special rigs to check the neck alignment while resetting the neck.

Jay also has a very fast, cheap method of repairing a loose neck joint on a guitar if the net worth of the guitar is less than the cost of hiring him to remove the neck, shim it, and replace it. He drills strategic holes, straps the neck in its proper position and fills the joint with what he calls *"real* epoxy." Apparently real epoxy is hard to get and most of the stuff labeled as epoxy for us common folk doesn't do the trick. This repair is permanent and there's no chance to ever reset the neck if it's not done right the first time. It's really too risky for amateurs and too much of a one-shot deal for a valuable instrument.

If you own a cheap guitar with a loose neck joint which you cannot afford to have repaired by a pro, proceed as follows.

You need to take off the strings, pry off the fingerboard (at least get it free of the body if not the neck), then lay the guitar, top down, on a padded work surface. I use a dining room chair. Pound on the heel with a mallet, using a pad (a book works nicely) to prevent marring the heel.

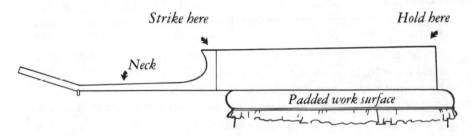

Strike here   *Hold here*

Neck

Padded work surface

The neck will slide out of its slot with a lot of horrible crunching sounds—the guitar body still amplifies sound. You then need to clean out the joint, chiselling out splinters and excess glue. Get some veneer to use as shims for the *sides* of the slot to make the joint *tight* upon reassembly. Use a good wood glue and a mallet to reassemble the joint. Let it sit overnight while the glue dries. Reinstall the fingerboard and begin adjusting the action.

A note on glue: Good old Elmer's white wood glue does a fine job. The only glue better for wood is a flesh-colored resin glue, like Tightbond (other companies make white and tan wood glues of similar quality. My intent is to specify *type* of glue and not brand). Epoxies and miracle bonding wonder glues generally cost more and are too brittle to hold any better than these cheaper glues on wood.

There are *other* kinds of neck joints, too. My candidate for

"Most Likely to Always Need Repair" can be distinguished by the absence of a heel and the presence of a plastic plate on the back of the guitar in the area of the neck block. Remove this plastic cover and you will find two or more large screws. That's all that holds the neck on.

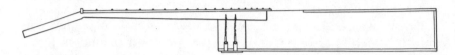

This is a misguided mechanical engineer's idea. Metal screws do not hold wood as well as glue. Wood swells and shinks with changes in relative humidity. Metal swells and shrinks much less, and it reacts to changes in temperature, not humidity.

When the furnace kicks on in a centrally heated home, the temperature rises, but the relative humidity falls. The wood shrinks and if the metal does anything, it expands. Motion like this patiently destroys the bond twixt metal and wood. Add string tension, which tries to tear the joint apart *anyway*, and you, like the guitar neck, shouldn't feel very secure.

Also note that a tapered dovetail joint fits such that it will almost take the string tension without glue, while the heel-less screw joint has no strength without the screws.

The playing action on guitars like this is typically hideous. It can be improved by removing the neck and shimming the joint either at the front or rear of the neck block and reassembling it, but such a repair is only temporary. In my opinion the best tool for repairing *this* kind of guitar is a lit match. First, stuff the soundbox full of newspaper . . .

A luthier friend has come up with yet another screw-on neck. He's especially proud of it. The holes go all the way through the neck block and two nuts are used through the soundhole to hold the neck on. It has the repair advantage of quick assembly/disassembly (about 2 minutes for each) and it is far superior to the other screw-on joint I just discussed. There is some mechanical strength to the joint even without the nuts, and the part which is to be repeatedly removed is a metal to metal union (nuts and bolts) and not a cruel, coarse screw tearing through the flesh of a

EXPLODED VIEW

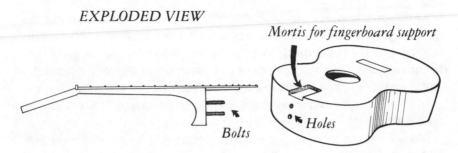

Mortis for fingerboard support

Bolts

Holes

defenseless dead tree. I believe the acoustics of the joint aren't as good as more traditional joints, and though it's much easier to repair, I think it would need repair more often.

If the neck itself breaks, or the tuning head splinters or separates from the neck, it's best to let a pro do the work. This often requires replacing wood and sometimes requires inventive joinery. A failed attempt on your part to repair it could really give a luthier trouble. Why?

When wood is broken there are fresh wood surfaces which may be glued back with proper clamping. If you glue it and fail to clamp or shim it properly, it leaves dried glue instead of fresh wood surface after your repair fails to hold. New glue doesn't stick to dried glue, so a repairperson needs to dig and scrape down to fresh wood.

I once saw a Fender acoustic 12-string guitar with a metal rod running the length of the body which could be seen clearly through the soundhole, but I didn't get the chance to get close enough to figure out what that design was all about. It was not one of my favorite instruments.

Body Repairs

It's even more advisable to have a luthier do repairs to the body than to the neck joint. Anything you do to the body affects the tone. Even changes in the finish change the tone. Don't take an old guitar in for refinishing like you'd take your car in for a new paint job, unless getting rid of scratches is worth getting back a guitar that sounds substantially and unpredictably different.

Dents are best left alone. Some folks lay a wet cloth over a dent and apply something like a soldering iron to the cloth so the steam swells the wood to pop out a dent. It works great on furniture. I've never tried it on a guitar, and somehow, approaching a guitar with a soldering iron bothers me more than cutting out a splinter from a sensitive area of a good friend. It hurts me to think about it.

Touchups to the finish and filling chipped places may be done, but matching the original comes best with experimentation and practice. I can't help you here except to suggest that you seek an experienced repairperson.

Small cracks with little or no gap can simply be filled with wood glue. Rub it in and wipe off all excess. The water in the glue will swell the wood and close the gap and the glue will hold it closed when it dries. Wider gaps may be filled with matching wooden shims glued into the crack, then cut, scraped or sanded flat to the original surface. This requires some refinishing, and I don't recommend it as an owner repair.

Cracks where one surface is higher than the other are a bit trickier, requiring internal patchwork. You almost certainly should pay to have a professional do it. One luthier friend recommends such patches (small pieces of wood glued crossgrain across the crack on the inside of the guitar) for repair of *all* cracks. He is admittedly a perfectionist and does superior work. I agree that patches are better, but it's not really something an owner would tend to do. Many repairpersons do not use patches unless the crack involves uneven surfaces.

If you have a loose brace inside the guitar, and you are as poor as I am, you can fix it without great skill. The problems are finding all of the loose areas of the brace(s), getting enough glue into the loose joint, and clamping the loose piece in place while the glue dries. And all this takes place inside your guitar.

To find loose areas, tap around the body, as described in the *test drive*. You can verify what you find by removing the strings and feeling around through the soundhole. Try to wiggle a brace that you suspect to be loose. If it comes off in your hand, it needed to be removed anyway. In that situation, applying the glue is simple. Dab glue onto the brace in your hand. Your problem *then* is getting the brace back to the right place, which can really be done only by practicing dry runs, feeling for where it was glued the first time.

If you can wiggle one end of the brace without it coming completely free, locating the brace is simple. It's already in place. Now your problem is getting glue into the joint. The best way is to use a hypodermic needle, which you might get from a doctor, nurse or lab technician. I've been told that, due to drug abuse, these needles are now illegal in the same way as prescription drugs, so you might have a minor hassle getting one. Laws such as these tend to restrict people with legitimate need of such articles, while a drug abuser is going to find a way to get them anyway. You may have to be as sneaky as a drug fiend. Nothing else works like a hypodermic.

The best clamp is so simple, it's amusing: a popsicle stick. Bend it, stick it into the soundhole, and place one end against the brace being glued and the other against the opposite surface of the guitar.

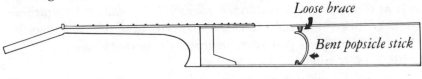

Loose brace

Bent popsicle stick

Use several sticks.

If your bridge comes off, it has to be mated well to the top—as flat or arched as the top. There must be *clean* (scraped) surfaces on both the bridge and the top. Placement is crucial if the guitar is going to play in tune, and it has to be clamped *tightly* with *good* wood glue. I highly recommend letting a pro do it.

The same goes for more hideous tasks such as broken necks or tuning heads, or the crushing or splintering of any area of the guitar requiring replacement of areas of wood. The average woodworker is not prepared to do this sort of thing. The delicate balance between strength and flexibility, and the accurate alignment of parts was difficult enough when the instrument was first built. It can be even harder to repair a guitar than to build one.

Tuning Machines

Some tuning machines are well made and permanently sealed, so even if you wanted to do some maintenance, you can't. Leave those alone unless something is obviously wrong with them, in which case you need a pro to fix or replace them.

Most guitars still have tuners with exposed gears. These require occasional lubrication and adjustment. A natural time to do this is when you change strings. Brand new guitars also often need it. While the string is off, use a little vaseline, or light machine oil, or powdered graphite (a pencil will do in a pinch) to coat the gears. It's also good to adjust any screws which hold the gears on their axles, but leave alone the little screws holding the mounting plates onto the tuning head. Adjustment is simple. Lightly try to turn the screw counterclockwise to check if it's loose (if it's tight, you don't need to loosen it), then turn it clockwise until it seats home (gets snug) and further tighten it very slightly. This will affect how stiff the tuning gear is to turn. You want it tight enough so that it doesn't slip, but loose enough for comfort. This adjustment is more difficult when the string is attached because the string tension puts pressure on the gear. Better to wait until the string is off (while changing strings).

Expensive sealed tuning machines locate this screw at the end of the tuning button. These days it is fashionable on cheaper guitars to make the normal inexpensive exposed gear tuners and then cover them. This gives you an inexpensive tuning machine which *looks* like an expensive sealed tuner. The problem is that it is *not* permanently lubricated and the tension screw is hidden under this useless, decorative cover.

You can recognize the cheap covered tuner by the absence of any sort of tension screw. The only screws you'll find are the mounting screws. To improve the guitar (though you'll make it slightly uglier), next time you've got a string off, remove the mounting screws to that tuning machine, remove the cover and dispose of it, replace the mounting screws, lubricate the tuning gears and adjust the tension screw.

If part of the tuning machine is broken, it's best to go to a music store or repairperson with guitar in hand, so you can both survey the situation, scratch chins and meditate on it. The problem is that tuning machines are anything but standardized. They come in all sizes, shapes and configurations. Seldom are parts interchangeable, and many guitars use machines you'd have a hard time tracking down. Also, if you are thinking about buying altogether new tuning machines, they all won't fit through the same holes. It's best to have the guitar and all the spare parts or tuning machine sets in one place for comparison.

CHAPTER 8

Acoustic Guitars and P.A. Systems

Some of you will probably want to perform with your instrument to crowds too large for your voice and guitar sounds to be heard without amplification. If you don't want to start playing an electric guitar, there are four common ways to amplify or *mic* an acoustic guitar.

First, you can play the guitar into a microphone. The problem here is that the best place for the microphone is about one inch from the strings, pointed directly into the soundhole; and that is usually where your right hand plays the strings. If you fingerpick, it often works best to locate the microphone just below your hand, pointing upward into the soundhole. That picks up sound well and also gives your audience a clear view of your dancing digits.

If you're a strummer, you'd probably hit a microphone in that position. It's best to keep the microphone about six inches away so your hand passes between it and the strings, or place the microphone out toward the fingerboard, pointing back toward the soundhole.

It would also work—though not as well—to point the microphone at the bridge. However you decide to try this technique,

check for feedback noises (screeches and whines) and change things around until something works. Also be aware that different microphones react in different ways to different rooms. You need to experiment.

FEEDBACK

Since I've mentioned feedback let me give you a little more information on it at this point. Feedback occurs with any P.A. system whenever the sound coming out of the speakers gets picked up by the microphone. The simplest way to get feedback (you do *not* want to do this) is to hold the microphone up to the speaker and turn up the volume. That's what the word comes from. The sound of the speaker "feeds back" into the microphone, getting re-amplified repeatedly until it's too loud for the system to handle.

A trickier way to get feedback is to bounce the sound of the speakers off something flat and smooth—like a wall or the top of a guitar—back into the microphone. This is the most common form of feedback and it's the most difficult to avoid when a loud volume is desired.

If you are choosing microphones and you don't know the difference between an omni-directional mic, uni-directional mic, or cardroid mic, it's best to go for the uni-directional or cardroid. Omni-directional mics pick up sound from any angle, while the others listen harder to what they're pointed at than what they're pointed away from. The way to use them is to point them at your guitar and away from the speakers.

Another sneaky means to attain feedback is to sit loud speakers on the same floor as the microphone stand. Solid floors carry sound even better than air—that's why Indian guides of old always put their ear to the ground to listen for approaching horses. So to avoid feedback from this source, it's good to place a thick towel or other cloth between the floor and the base of the microphone stand. This also allows you to tap your foot while playing without blasting the first three rows of audience out of their chairs.

Yet another form of feedback occurs when an extremely loud amplifier makes the flat face of an acoustic guitar vibrate, producing a very muddy, booming sound when you play bass notes. Some performers avoid this by taping cardboard over the soundhole of their guitar. Flat black cardboard is aesthetically better than white.

Enough on feedback, back to ways to amplify your guitar. **Contact microphones** or **transducers** are specially built to be glued to a surface, such as a guitar bridge. The glue is a substance similar to a wad of chewing gum, so it can be relocated or removed without demaging the guitar. They pick up the sound of the surface without picking up much of the sound from the air around the microphone. Glued to the guitar bridge, or the soundboard near the bridge, a contact microphone is less likely to feed back than a regular mic on a stand. It's also less awkward.

The disadvantage of a contact mic is that it must be attached to a part of your guitar that vibrates a lot. This adds weight to that vibrating surface, slightly altering the sound. If you *love* the tone of your guitar, you might not want to change it by adding a contact mic.

Contact mics vary in design. Some are round and some are rectangular, but they are all rather small. Some are designed to be glued to the bridge and have an adhesive backing already in place.

Some have volume controls and tone controls, which are not really necessary because most amplifiers already have them.

For those who don't want a little black box with a dangling cord glued to the outside of their guitar, there are contact mics designed to go inside the guitar. This type is typically glued to the underside of the bridge area and is wired so you may plug your amp into the tailpin of your guitar. Aesthetically this is nicer, but you should get a luthier to install such a mic.

The best way to properly locate a transducer is by experimentation. Try it in several locations on the bridge and top and decide which spot gives your P.A. the best sound.

Magnetic pickups are the third alternative. They mount in the soundhole and because they do not add weight to any vibrating parts of the guitar, they don't change the acoustic sound of the guitar at all. The drawback is that the electric sound sent to the amplifier has little resemblance to the acoustic sound of the guitar. Adding such a pickup basically converts an acoustic guitar to an electric one Ideally, it would probably be better to get two guitars: one electric and one acoustic. An electric guitar is better than an acoustic guitar with a magnetic pickup.

Your last alternative is a piezo-electric pickup. Ovation guitars feature such a pickup built into the bridge on some of their guitars. Piezo-electric basically means that if you hit certain rocks with a hammer, they give off a little spark of electricity. These rocks or *crystals* give off more subtle electric charges if they are merely squeezed. Pressure makes them electrified.

These guitars have little crystals planted under each string at the bridge. As each string vibrates, it exerts pressure in pulses to each of these crystals. The crystals send their pulsing electric charges through wires toward the amplifier. This design basically combines the disadvantages of contact microphones and magnetic ones. The weight affects the acoustic tone and the electric sound has little to do with the acoustic tone. What you end up with can only be described as an Ovation guitar. If you like the sound of an Ovation, go for it. There's nothing else like it.

Guitar companies often imitate Martins. They seldom imitate Ovations. That suggests something about the unique Ovation sound. Thus speaks a very opinionated observer.

In recent years newer designs for built-in contact mics have appeared which advertise that they do not damage the acoustic properties of the guitars in which they are mounted. Their basic change is that they try to attach only a *very* light portion of their microphone to the soundboard, with heavier parts mounted on the sides of the guitar where mass and weight are less important to tone. It makes sense to me, though I've only seen it available already built into certain guitars, and I haven't been able to test any of these intruments. At this point it's pretty much *state-of-the-art* and expensive. If you have the money, you might look for it in larger guitar shops in larger cities. Guitar-oriented magazines offer more up-to-date info on state-of-the-art if that's what you are into. Look at ads and reviews. The words you are now reading might already be a few years old, and that might not be state-of-the-art.

Whatever type of microphone or pickup you buy, it always makes sense to test it out first before buying. Listen carefully and bring a friend along to discuss it. Discussing it with the salesperson usually results in buying it whether it's what you want or not.

CHAPTER 9

Electric Guitars: A Brief Intro

As with the acoustic guitar, the sound of an electric guitar starts with the vibrating string. Rather than using the motion of the vibrations to pump a wooden membrane—the soundboard—in and out to amplify the sound, the motion of the electric guitar's strings interferes with the small magnetic field surrounding a magnetic pickup. This interference creates an electrical pulse in the fine coils of wire in the pickup. The amplitude and quality of these pulses are altered by volume and tone controls on the guitar before being transmitted through a cable to an electronic amplifier. The amplifier further changes the pulses and increases the amplitude to pump speaker cones in and out, creating the tones which shatter glass, eardrums, and the hearts of lovesick teenagers.

Like acoustic guitars, the electronic counterpart has a neck, tuning head and tuning gears. The fingerboard often is longer, with more frets than an acoustic guitar, and the playing action is typically much lower than an acoustic steel-string guitar. The neck is usually screwed onto the body in a fashion similar to the screw-on acoustic neck which, as you now know, I like least.

The body of an electric guitar is most often a solid or laminated

SOLID BODY ELECTRIC GUITAR

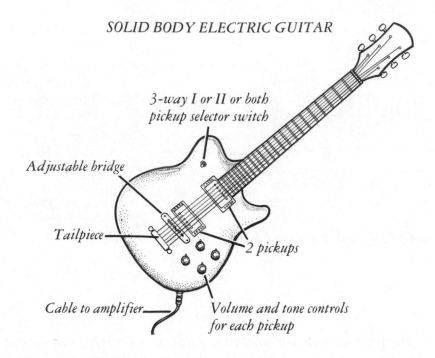

*3-way I or II or both
pickup selector switch*

Adjustable bridge

Tailpiece

2 pickups

Cable to amplifier

*Volume and tone controls
for each pickup*

block of hardwood. It's shape has nothing to do with the sound, though the heavier the body, the longer the notes the guitar will sustain.

Some electric guitars are *hollow bodied*, meaning they have a body similar to an arch top acoustic guitar, though it's usually much smaller and thinner, and the acoustic volume is a bit puny. The acoustic body affects the vibration of the string and so affects the sound emitted from the speakers.

A while back, players noticed that if you play a hollow-body electric guitar very loudly, the screaming tone coming from the speaker would force the thin acoustic top to vibrate. The vibration carried through the bridge onto the strings, which were the source of the screaming tone coming out of the speakers. The speakers amplified the strings which amplified the speakers which . . . As described in the last chapter, it's called feedback, and it sounds terrible.

To give guitarists that hollow-body electric sound with less feedback problems, a newer design was created called the *semi-*

hollow body electric guitar. It is a stiffer, heavier body than a hollow body.

An adjustable bridge does less harm to the tone of an electric guitar than to an acoustic guitar, because the bridge serves only to give a solid anchor to that end of the string. It doesn't conduct sound energy to the body, so it doesn't hurt if it's heavy. Many electric guitars have bridges with separate saddles for each string. Each saddle adjusts to a separate string length to properly set the intonation for each string.

Most electric guitars now have two pickups. One is near the bridge while the other is near the end of the fingerboard. Because they pick up a different section of the vibrating strings, each pickup has a separate image of the string's vibration, with the sound differing between them. To use that difference, most guitars have a pickup selector switch. The up, middle, and down positions of this switch give you the sound of one pickup alone, both pickups, or the second pickup alone. A player may decide that one pickup sounds better for rhythmic backup while the combination sings out for a solo riff. The convenient positioning of the switch allows a change even in the middle of a riff. (A riff is what an electric guitarist is doing in a rock n' roll song when nobody is singing and the spotlight is on the guitarist who is making faces, jumping, twisting, writhing, sweating and generally acting like he or she and the guitar are each trying to strangle the other. All you hear is the random wails of the guitar, accompanied by the even, rhythmic thump of the bass and drums.)

Electric guitars are often associated with very loud noises. Neighbors and family members sometimes grow to associate it with homicidal fantasies. Though it's best to blast the open air to blend with an electric bass, drums and/or synthesizers and other keyboards, when you practice alone, you might consider ways to blast your own ears without invading public airspace. You can get practice headphones and miniature amps which give you all the noise at a fraction of the volume. It is possible to play an electric guitar through a home stereo by plugging it into a tape deck's microphone jack while the deck monitor is switched to "line." On cheaper decks, you'll need to press the *record* button. On *any* deck, you'll need to begin with *all* of the volume controls turned all the way down, lest you blow out the circuits of the deck or the amp or the speakers. An electric guitar's output is a lot higher than the average microphone. Slowly and carefully play the guitar while watching the meters on the tape deck. If they are dead, turn up the volume *slightly*. Play some more. This goes for both the volume controls on the guitar and the tape deck.

Choosing an Electric Guitar

It's best to use the same principles as in choosing an acoustic guitar. Bring a friend. Check out the action. Wear it and see if it suits you. The additional important thing is to plug the guitar in and listen to it. It is *best* to plug it into the same amp you'll be playing it through, so you don't sound better in the store than you do at home.

Used electric guitars are checked out just like used acoustic guitars, except again, plug it in and listen, especially if you can hear it through the system you will be using.

There are many gadgets and "effects" boxes for electric guitars. Each one changes the sound of your instrument. Fuzz boxes or overload boxes basically distort the sound as if you had the volume all the way up, giving you the option of that tone without having the volume all the way up. Flangers are usually echo boxes, especially if it echoes only once. Echoplex and other reverb units also add echoes and faster reverberations. The only way to know if you want any of these is to plug your guitar into each and listen. You must decide if it's worth the price to make your guitar sound like that.

Electric guitar strings are made with special magnetic cores. Aside from different tones from each brand (a matter of personal preference), you may wish to choose different gauge strings depending on your style of playing. If you like to bend notes by stretching the strings to the side, you will prefer lighter gauge strings. If you tend to play rhythm guitar and want to play whole chords which are in tune, you will prefer heavier gauge strings. Lighter gauge strings, stretch so easily that you may accidentally bend notes out of tune, while heavier gauge strings are painful to bend.

CHAPTER 10

Conclusion

Well, friends, that pretty much covers the wholeness of guitar-ness as I understand it—unless I've forgotten something. I'm *sure* I've forgotten *something*. This book is intended to help you understand your guitar. By now you should certainly understand it better than you did before you read my words of wisdom.

The only thing left is learning to play this object of understand-ing. The most ideal situation is having a friend who plays exactly like you want to play, who is also just dying to show you how—for free. Unfortunately, most of us don't have that situation. Next best is a good teacher who will do it for a reasonable fee. Finding one is usually easy. Just ask around at music stores, colleges and at gatherings of musicians.

If you either can't find a teacher or don't have the cash to hire one, there are many books on guitar playing in almost any style. You can find a good selection at either music or book stores. Take along a musician friend to help you select a good music method book. Generally, you should look for a book which offers songs you want to learn. If it's full of "Mary Had a Little Lamb" or "Home on the Range," you might be wasting your money. If it is a songbook and includes nothing about how to play, it may also be a waste of money until you learn how to learn a song from a songbook.

Originally this book was to include an introduction to playing the guitar, but it was decided to leave it out. There are so many different styles of playing and so many good method books out for each style that many people buying this book would use only the "Owners Manual" half. Without the music section, the book is more affordable and serves more people.

If you are one of those folks who wouldn't have wanted my contribution to the already existing glut of guitar method books · on the market, I hope this book has served you well. If, however, you've become uniquely pleased by my particular style of explaining things and would want a method book written by me, you ought to write and say so: Will Martin, c/o John Muir Publications, P.O. Box 613, Santa Fe, NM 87501.

If they get thousands of requests from readers who really would want such a book, it will happen. Otherwise, it won't. It would include an introduction and development of fingerpicking techniques and flatpicking techniques for folk guitar, and some classic guitar techniques as well. It would go over basic music theory and show you how to learn songs from other songbooks by teaching you how to read tablature, treble clef and bass clef. It would also have a lot of songs in it that you couldn't get anywhere else—because I wrote them. There would also be a little help for those who are interested in writing their own songs. You should also feel free to write with any questions or comments you wish to make about this book already in your hands. We hope there will be later editions, and your remarks might improve them. I may even answer you directly, if I can afford the stamps.

There's an ancient piece of music which is written so that the ending is just the beginning played backwards. It is called "My End Is My Beginning." My college roommate did a version for two musicians facing each other reading the same sheet of music lying flat between them. He called it "My End Is *Your* Beginning."

That's what I'd like to think is true of this book and your enjoyment of the guitar. Get hungry. Get other books. Each teacher will have something different to offer.

Music is a celebration of life. Playing it is better than just listening because it makes you part of the experience instead of merely an observer. Live, love, and be happy.

My end is your beginning.

Additional copies of *The Guitar Owner's Manual* may be ordered by filling out the form below and enclosing $6.95 plus $1 postage & handling. Send your order to:

John Muir Publications
P.O. Box 613
Santa Fe, NM 87501

JOHN MUIR PUBLICATIONS
P.O. Box 613   SANTA FE, NM 87501

Enclosed is $_____ for _____ copies of *The Guitar Owner's Manual* @ $6.95 each plus $1 postage & handling. Please send to:

NAME _____

ADDRESS _____

CITY _____ STATE _____ ZIP _____

(Allow 3 weeks for delivery)